The Commu... Organisation

Michael Blakstad joined the BBC as a general trainee in 1962 and soon began to specialise in producing scientific and technical programmes such as *Horizon*. He edited *Tomorrow's World* for six years and later devised an award-winning series about industry, *The Risk Business*. In 1980 he became the first director of programmes at Television South. He has written two previous books and numerous articles for business and design publications. He founded Workhouse in 1984 and is its Chief Executive.

Aldwyn Cooper studied Psychology at London University, obtained a PhD in theories of learning and conducted further research in California on psychology, statistics and artificial intelligence. In 1980 he joined Henley – The Management College, where he established the pioneering distance-learning programme. He became professor of management studies at Henley/Brunel, carried out HRD consultancy assignments throughout the world and took up a position on the board of the Open College in 1987. He was appointed managing director of Workhouse in 1993.

Workhouse has its own editing and DTP facilities, and now designs and produces communications programmes for a wide range of blue-chip organisations such as Barclays, Railtrack, Price Waterhouse, Courtaulds, Nuclear Electric and BAA; this book draws largely on the experience gained from such accounts. The company also makes around a hundred hours of documentary, educational and children's television each year.

The Communicating Organisation

Michael Blakstad
and
Aldwyn Cooper

INSTITUTE OF PERSONNEL
AND DEVELOPMENT

Typeset by Photoprint, Torquay
Printed in Great Britain by
The Short Run Press, Exeter

British Library Cataloguing in Publication Data

A catalogue record for this book is available from the British Library

ISBN 0–85292–575–1

The views expressed in this book are the authors' own, and may not necessarily reflect those of the IPD.

**INSTITUTE OF PERSONNEL
AND DEVELOPMENT**

IPD House, Camp Road, London SW19 4UX
Tel: 0181 971 9000
Registered office as above. Registered Charity No. 1038333
A company limited by guarantee. Registered in England No. 2931892

Contents

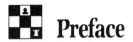 **Preface**

Who controls communications with your people in your organisation? The unions – as they did with management's acquiescence when I first joined BT? Before that I had been director of personnel at the BBC where staff usually read about corporation affairs in the *Guardian* or the trade press long before management is able to get the message through the official channels. Then there's the grapevine – the most virulent of all networks. If you can truly say that management is first with the news, then your company is one of the very few.

Employee communications are only now surfacing as a branch of management skills which can be identified and learned. It is no more than a decade or so since most companies came to terms with *external* communications and the skills needed to handle the media or to promote their company and its products or services to outside audiences. In the 1990s they are coming for the first time to appreciate that there is an equal and opposite discipline involved in internal communications.

As they do so, they are finding their own people harder to convince than the slippery customers of television and the press. Staff know more about the company than journalists; there is less chance of passing them off with partial information or simple 'no comments'.

While I was chief executive of BT UK during the period of privatisation and immediately after, I chose to become closely involved in communicating the company's message both inside and outside the organisation. As President of the IPD, I am anxious that directors and managers understand the importance and the techniques of talking with, not simply at, their people. That's why I agreed to become chairman of a relatively small company in Winchester whose service to its clients is helping them communicate – to television audiences through its broadcast work and to their own people through its Corporate division.

The two principals of that firm have written this book, the first to attempt to draw together the lessons learned by some of Britain's leading organisations in their own endeavours in employee communication. It is to be hoped that the book will be read and absorbed not only by managers with direct responsibility for internal communications but by senior executives whose job it is to formulate strategies and ensure that they are implemented.

Michael Blakstad and Aldwyn Cooper have asked me to acknowledge many others in their team whose work has contributed significantly to the development of the basic rules described in *The Communicating Organisation*, and especially to Chris Grayling, the Head of Corporate Programmes whose own work with such companies as Railtrack and Courtaulds is reported in these pages.

Finally, a word of thanks is due to the organisations which have agreed to allow their activities to be reported in this book. Only if the pioneers are prepared to be honest about their failures as well as their successes can the next wave of communicators hope to avoid the pitfalls encountered in the past.

Mike Bett, President,
Institute of Personnel and Development

Introduction

The Communicating Organisation came to be written because Matthew Reisz, commissioning editor at the Institute of Personnel Management (now the Institute of Personnel and Development) had spotted an article in the *Director* magazine. The article described and gently criticised the efforts of the BBC to communicate its radical new policy, Producer Choice, to its staff.

There can be few workforces anywhere in the world more difficult to persuade to change their ways than the turbulent priests and priestesses of broadcasting; in this case, the Director General John Birt was introducing drastic changes to the tenets and practice of their whole religion.

The article suggested that the BBC could have learned from the experience of others, including some of the organisations whose stories are told in these pages. Matthew Reisz contacted the writer, Michael Blakstad, and invited him to expand this experience into a handbook for boards and managers who face similar challenges.

The *Director* article had described other companies for which Blakstad and his colleagues had worked in helping them communicate different forms of change programmes. His company, Workhouse, had started life as a television and video company. At first, the company used its television skills to create so-called corporate videos – mainly for external audiences promoting the company or its products. By the start of the 1990s Workhouse had become concerned by the limitations of video as a means of corporate communication and sensed that the medium was coming to be regarded – in an increasingly harsh economic environment – as an expensive and ineffective means of communication.

The company's response was to commission one of the research studies described in Chapter 2. The findings led Workhouse to a radical re-design of the media it produced for employee communications programmes. As part of the re-engineering of its product, the company recruited an experienced guru from the world of management training, Dr Aldwyn Cooper, the co-author of this book. The research findings also indicated that media other than video were essential; Workhouse had developed desktop publishing facilities and was producing printed materials, slides and audio programmes as well as video.

Other companies, too, were developing niche skills in the arena of employee communications. Meanwhile, some large organisations were starting to identify the need to appoint specialist internal communications managers. Until then, the task of spreading company messages to their staff had fallen indiscriminately either to the personnel department or to the corporate communications/affairs unit, two disciplines with radically different traditions and ways of working, as we shall see in Chapter 2. Very few had dedicated budgets for employee communications, with the result that every campaign had to be tackled as a special project.

Workhouse was fortunate in having a number of clients, with whom it had been working for some years, who were willing to listen to the results of our research findings and to the expertise of its newly recruited guru. Nuclear Electric, Price Waterhouse and Rover were among the first to acknowledge the logic of the new approach and their experiences are reported in the book.

One by one, new companies also dipped their toes in the unfamiliar waters. Meridian Broadcasting already knew enough about television to accept our recommendations for including it alongside other media, making its employee communications much more effective than video on its own.

United Distillers was guided by an external consultant. Greg Spiro knew that if he was to extend the reach of UD's new culture he needed the help which media could provide; he adopted a mixed-media approach which made it possible to spread the word before the new corporate philosophy became grounded by its own weight and complexity.

By now, enough experience had been gained to allow the authors to compare notes and discuss results not only with

Workhouse clients but with others who had built a reputation for their own pioneering work in the field of employee communications – BP, IBM, BT and AEA Technology are some that have kindly allowed us to report their experiences.

When Workhouse first decided to spread the word about its new approach to employee communications it was encouraged by its design company, The Partners, to distil its experience into a series of brief rule books ('the five rules of communications') which are probably the shortest rule books ever published – none of them takes more than three minutes to read! The rule books led to the article in *Director* magazine . . . and this book was conceived.

The rules are deceptively simple – only by reading the case studies reported in this book will you appreciate how difficult they are to apply. But they create the context in which this book is written and it will be helpful to spell them out here:

- **Plot your route** – what must be done even before a communications programme begins.
- **Shoot the pianist** – forget the old routines and design your programme around the answers.
- **Enrol your owners** – get the audience so involved that they end up by owning the message.
- **Encourage positive heckling** – how to get feedback.
- **Count the cost** – how to avoid the opposite dangers of spending too little and too much.

There is a danger in formulating rules; it can give the impression that the desired outcome will be guaranteed if the rules are followed. The greatest paradox surrounding corporate communications – internal or external – lies in the fact that information will always be a two-edged sword. Both too little and too much knowledge can be dangerous things – and it is devilishly difficult to decide in advance just how much information is the right amount.

You will read in this book of a Chief Executive who didn't match the culture he was attempting to communicate to his staff; another Chairman / Chief Executive was removed by his Board partly because the change programme he had introduced proved too turbulent – and because he had failed to enlist the support of his most senior colleagues. The inherent danger which accompanies communication is reflected in our dedication of this book to the new heroes of the business world, the communications managers. In their name we offer you this rudimentary map of the minefield.

1

Dramatis Personae – The Communications Manager as Hero

Change is now endemic in successful organisations; companies are faced with the need for constant change if they are to stay abreast of the needs of their customers, new technologies, increasing competition, the expectations of the workforce and the whole armoury of pressures which have laid siege to the boardroom and the management committee.

Consultants are benefiting from the boom. External consultants earn their fees by applying specialist poultices to the rash of uncertainty, techniques like business process re-engineering, open systems, just-in-time production methods, non-financial performance measurements and the rest. Internal consultants, too, help guide their companies towards new strategies, missions and cultures.

Alas, all too many well-designed change management programmes fail to achieve their full potential because the message is not properly communicated to the people whose support and ownership is needed to implement the new strategy. Many a consultant's recommendation is doomed to bite the dust unseen by the majority of the company's staff; all too often, the most logical policies fade into inertia only one or two layers away from the executive team which commissioned and agreed them.

This book is about an emerging breed of business hero – the employee communications manager. Emerging, because few organisations have segregated the internal communication role from that of external relations. Heroic, because communications is a powerful explosive with an unpredictable fuse. Properly planned and implemented, the results can unclog rusty channels and get the company's juices flowing. Often, the flame sputters and dies. Just occasionally, the explosive goes off in the faces of the team which lit the fuse.

1

We report a series of case studies of companies and firms that have bravely undertaken the challenge of communicating important and often complex messages to their entire workforce. In particular, we observe how new strategies or corporate philosophies have been communicated by these companies – with varying degrees of success. Within the context of these change programmes we concentrate in particular on the people responsible for managing communication and the tools they chose.

The case studies are fascinating because they reveal how a varied group of organisations have come to design new strategies by which to guide their workforces. We feature the inside stories of company directors and senior executives who have faced up to the need for change in the worlds of chemicals, liquor, television, car manufacture, the nuclear industry, oil, telecommunications, computing and consultancy.

The book describes the means deployed by these organisations in rolling out their strategies, policies and cultures to their employees and, in some cases, to the 'extended family' of suppliers, customers and investors. The case studies offer opportunities for managers in any branch of business to benchmark, to spot similarities between their needs and those of our 'heroes', between common challenges faced in transmitting any message through layers of people, locations and interests which comprise corporate life today, between costs, budgets and success factors. For some, the case studies may serve as bench-marks of best practice; bear in mind that no two cases are the same, any more than any two companies or firms are identical.

Employee communication is a new and emerging business discipline; there are as yet few universal rules which can be applied. None the less, we attempt at the end of the book to draw up a number of guidelines which we believe will help people responsible for employee communications to draw up their own plans of campaign (see Chapter 8). They may decide not to follow all the rules we have drafted; they will at least have had the chance to consider the reasons why these companies succeeded or failed and make their own choice in the light of the experience of others.

We start our odyssey with a research report; Chapter 2 offers a summary of the findings of three studies conducted into employee communications. These surveys throw light on organisational issues, for instance the position occupied by internal communications managers within the management structures of different companies – and the budgets allocated to them. They reflect the opinions of communications managers on the various media and techniques available to them. They also report on the ways in which experienced and successful practitioners design and use the tools at their disposal. Finally, they reflect the attitude of executives to the forms in which messages should reach them. The chapter also draws on the findings of cognitive research to indicate how communications programmes can be designed to embrace such techniques as the effort theory of learning, and ensure that their message is truly received and understood.

Chapter 3 – Plot Your Route – is dedicated to the essential groundwork which should precede any major employee communications campaign – defining the message, and in particular, researching the audience. We describe how one company, AEA Technology, has systematically investigated the perceptions of people inside and outside the organisation and, on these findings, built not only a communications policy but also a strategy for the whole organisation as it stepped out along the path to privatisation. We also show how Price Waterhouse Management Consultancy Services turned its magnifying glass upon itself and how it planned a three-year communications campaign designed to unify its divided partnership and demoralised staff.

Chapter 4 sets out the second Workhouse rule of communication – Shoot the Pianist – which argues that the old tunes should be abandoned. There are new symphonies to be played on a variety of instruments, which must be meticulously orchestrated and rehearsed. United Distillers embarked on a hugely ambitious communications exercise in an attempt to

unify the culture of its operations in 35 countries. Following a
full year of face-to-face briefings with the group's top 1,000
executives around the world, the company then set about
communicating 'The UD Way' to the rest of the company's
15,000 staff. It used the full range of communications tools,
adapted to local cultures, carefully planned to ensure that
enough time and resources were dedicated to discussion and
feedback. There was, however, a twist in the tale – UD's chief
executive was replaced before the programme was fully under-
way, and the campaign was stalled pending the arrival of a new
boss, and a new tune to play.

In the same chapter we recount how Rover Cars transformed itself; Britain's last national car manufacturer became a
byword for change management. The company was losing
taxpayers' money hand over fist until it was peremptorily sold
to British Aerospace at a figure so low it later fell foul of the
EC's competition law. Under its new Chairman, Graham Day,
the company embarked on a root-and-branch upheaval of old
working methods, borrowing the best of Japanese manufacturing methods but above all involving its workforce at every
stage. Its leadership walked the talk, putting into practice the
principles it was introducing. The change programme emerged
intact from yet another change of ownership, BMW's purchase
of Rover Cars from British Aerospace, and the company is
now famous for quality and cost-effectiveness.

Chapter 5 – Enrol Your Owners – pin-points the need to
identify, train and brief the people who will communicate the
message. British Petroleum's famous 'Project 1990' failed in
some of its goals (and possibly hastened the departure of its
then Chairman and Chief Executive Robert Horton) but
succeeded in creating the most important ingredient of all, a
teamworking culture throughout the organisation, by means of
which senior management can be confident that the message is
really reaching every level of staff.

Courtaulds represents a large number of manufacturing
companies whose workforces operate shifts and present a
formidable communications challenge. Courtaulds was mer-

ging its English and Spanish viscose and acrylics operations with those of Hoechst in Germany; it needed to allay the fears generated by any business merger whilst motivating staff in all three countries to absorb and deliver the strategy of the joint venture. It too designed and implemented crash programmes which helped create a clear identity and focus for their enterprises; in the UK, in particular, it was able to tap into an effective cell-briefing network which the company had established some years earlier, and was able to enlist its line managers to lead the process.

When Meridian Broadcasting was granted its licence to broadcast in the south and south-east of England it had just 14 months to recruit its entire staff and mould them into a homogeneous unit. It relied on a small project team to design a mixed-media introductory briefing course and then called on the same people to facilitate seminars for everyone joining the new company.

Chapter 6 – Selecting the Media – demonstrates how companies can call on media to improve the effectiveness of employee communications. In particular, the media place policies firmly on the record, and thus ensure that the message remains consistent as it passes through a number of ears and mouths.

Railtrack succeeded in communicating with every signalman within hours of reaching outline agreement with the RMT in order to explain the terms of the complex proposals; the ensuing vote ensured the end of the expensive and disruptive dispute. Nuclear Electric created a complete 'tool-kit' for its representatives in rolling out a complex and controversial message. The company needed an effective communications campaign in order to fight for its very existence in the face of the government's review of its nuclear policy. It had to convey its complex case to a small but vitally influential group of opinion formers, politicians and supporters. Nuclear Electric built a carefully structured programme, using the media of print, audio and video each to perform the task for which it is best equipped. It harnessed the persuasive powers of a cadre of

communicators within its own ranks – the so-called Talks
Service – and, in briefing them, unexpectedly unleashed a
powerful employee communications exercise.

Chapter 7 – We Have the Technology – examines the new
technologies which are making communications ever more
effective when they are properly harnessed. We see how two of
the largest purveyors of communications equipment, BT and
IBM, have deployed their own telecommunications and
computer networks in order to reach their own staff during
periods when both companies have been obliged radically to
overhaul their organisations and ways of working.

In chapter 8 – Count the Cost – we review our own rules and
attempt to establish guidelines for those who are about to start
employee communications programmes in their organisations.
There is no single prescription for success; every company and
every message is different. However, if you don't even
consider which of these rules will apply to your company you
might just as well throw into the nearest incinerator the money
and resources you are about to spend on preparing your
employee communications. There are lessons to be learned
from the mistakes which our heroes admit to having made; and
there are many more aspects of employee communications
where analysis has still to be done and the results analysed.

To show how high is the mountain still to be climbed, it is
sobering to consider that of the cases we report in this book,
fewer than half can be described as out-and-out success stories.
A tribute is due to the companies and firms that have allowed
us to revisit episodes in their history some would sooner forget.
Only by allowing their experiences to be shared with others can
mistakes be avoided in the future.

 # The Research

In the early 1990s change management was the hot topic at business schools and in the boardrooms of embattled corporations. In the mid-1990s senior management are learning that communication is intrinsic to change management; the best strategy in the world is ineffective unless it is properly communicated to the people whose support is needed to effect the new policies.

Communication skills are moving to the front of the management agenda. But what exactly are these skills? Not just the ability to make speeches and wow the shareholders. Communication now comprises a set of techniques which are, perhaps for the first time, being defined and measured. Employee communications now has its own association, the ECA, an adjunct of the Industrial Society. There will soon be more and more lecturers in communications skills at business schools and regular conferences to share the latest experience. However, in order to establish a proper discipline, there needs to be a body of agreement on topics such as best practice and measurable effectiveness.

That can't be done without scientific research, and this chapter reports on a number of studies which have been commissioned either by such august bodies as the Industrial Society and the CBI or by our company Workhouse.

The CBI study was conducted by the Business Research Unit as background to a communications campaign aimed at chief executives. The CBI wanted to convey the important message that CEOs were responsible above all else for the competitive strategies of their companies. Michael Blakstad was Editorial Director of the project and it was essential that the team was certain about the most suitable format in which to package the message. CEOs are notoriously short of time and patience; they have learned to ration their time and concentrate on the heart of the matter. The CBI study provided important and surprising guidance for briefing these busy discriminating managers.

The purpose behind the study commissioned by Workhouse was very specific, centred as it was on the use of media in communications. Workhouse had been established as a production company pure and simple, making television programmes and corporate videos. We had an uneasy feeling that video as a medium was held in low esteem by most corporate communicators – not so much the poor relation as the fat cat which had eaten the cream and was now slumped extravagantly in the corner.

The study conducted by Quadrangle examined ways in which professional communicators use different media (including audio, text, slides and – most important of all – the human facilitator). Research was confined to people who earn their living training or communicating within companies and it asked questions of fact – how these people actually behave – not opinion or theory.

Another study was conducted by MORI and it surveyed members of the Industrial Society; MORI too researched what companies actually do, not what they think people should do. Interestingly, the MORI study gave an indication of companies' spending on communications. Only 28 per cent of the companies surveyed had a separate budget for communications and this part of the survey is confined to that sample; these companies spend an annual average of £290.00 per head on communicating with their employees (see Figure 2.1), and up to £2,000 in some cases. The highest spending falls to companies with over 1,000 employees – £382.00 – and if those with over 2,500 staff spend less than that per head that is presumably simply because they command economies of scale. So we're looking at a sizeable number of companies which spend upwards of £300,000 on employee communications and some which spend millions.

By far the most common, and highly rated, channel for

Figure 2.1

Spending on employee communications

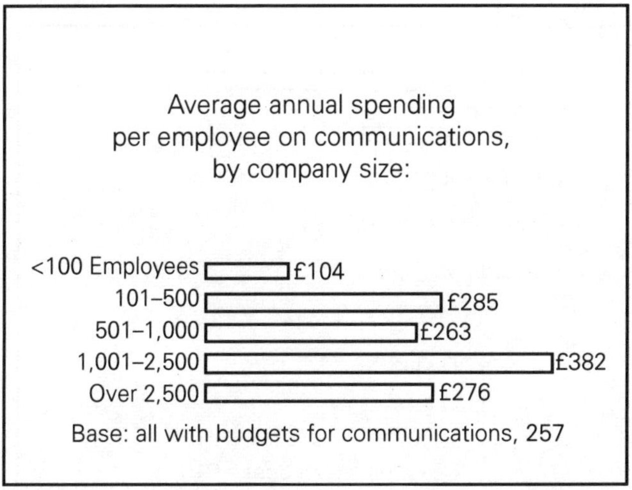

Average annual spending
per employee on communications,
by company size:

<100 Employees ☐☐☐ £104
101–500 ☐☐☐☐☐☐ £285
501–1,000 ☐☐☐☐☐ £263
1,001–2,500 ☐☐☐☐☐☐☐☐ £382
Over 2,500 ☐☐☐☐☐☐ £276

Base: all with budgets for communications, 257

communicating with employees is team briefings (see Figure 2.2). Electronic media, such as e-mail and video, come low on the scale. It is possible that this finding reflects the conservatism of the Industrial Society's membership, but it would be wrong to ignore the antagonism caused by inappropriate video programmes and by impersonal messages left blinking on the e-mail screen.

When it comes to hearing the opinions of the workforce, team briefing is again the most highly rated, along with 'walking the job'.

This would appear to be a further example of the interesting results from the much quoted 'Hawthorne' study carried out at the Western Electrical Company in the late 1930s and corroborated in many further studies since. The Hawthorne study showed that a positive effect is nearly always gained by a company demonstrating that it is taking 'genuine interest' in the workforce. A team briefing involving peers and managers is a far more overt form of interest than an impersonal piece of video, a newsletter or an e-mail file.

Figure 2.2
*The most highly rated channels for communicating
with employees*

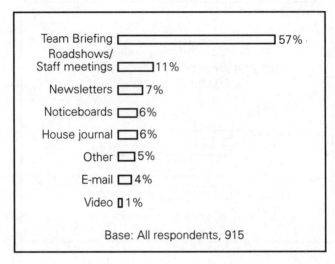

There are two other observations from these types of study that are worthy of note. The first is that, provided that the briefing is well constructed and delivered there is often a positive improvement in performance after team briefings even when the message is essentially negative. People have complex motivations in the workplace and the need to be well informed and involved is one of them. The second is that any positive effect of team briefing is rapidly lost if the process is not maintained as part of a more consistent and planned exercise. Indeed, it can be the case that the net effect becomes negative if the apparent involvement of the workforce is not maintained.

The Industrial Society survey also asked where in each organisation the ultimate responsibility lies for employee communications. Influenced, perhaps, by the background from which many of the Society's members have emerged, 62 per cent of the communications managers surveyed answer to the personnel function in their company (see Figure 2.3). This

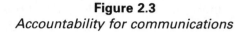

Figure 2.3
Accountability for communications

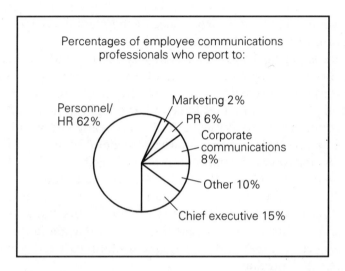

contrasts with the pattern detected by the study Workhouse commissioned a couple of years earlier, where communication fell almost equally to the human resources and to the public relations functions, with marketing and other offices holding sway in a minority of companies.

The involvement of public relations and marketing had arisen, presumably, because communications had traditionally been seen as the art of influencing external audiences; these were the people who understood media and worked with external suppliers like ourselves. Personnel and human resource development functions had fallen to managers who are more familiar with such techniques as assessment interviews, team briefings and group negotiations. Furthermore, their budgets were considerably less generous than those of the influencers. Since employee communications was a mystery to most boards, companies allocated its responsibility more or less randomly between the two disciplines.

Workhouse's own experience reflects this schism; the people who commission us to help communicate large-scale corporate change come more or less equally from both disciplines. Frequently, we find ourselves working with both directorates at once. As might be expected, those with PR and marketing backgrounds have more experience of the media and need less persuasion to invest the necessary funds.

There is perhaps another reason why the PR and marketing functions have become more involved in internal communications as well as seeking to communicate to external audiences. More and more companies have either sought to involve their own suppliers more directly in the company's key cultural values or are seeking to outsource considerably more of their supplies and services from external organisations which have often been set up by staff who have been made redundant or who have taken early retirement. The essential 'internal communications' are no longer restricted within the walls of the company itself but are reaching a far wider audience who are subject to other influences and sometimes need a more sophisticated product.

The Quadrangle survey also drew attention to the distinction which most companies drew between training and human resource development. Training applied to the operatives and used, basically, *teaching* techniques. HRD applied to management grades and involved *learning* principles.

Like the Industrial Society, Quadrangle perceived hostility to electronic media and particularly video, stemming in part from the training–HRD distinction – the big bucks and the flashy technology had largely been directed at clients or influencers; the techniques used in promotional videos are unsuited to internal communications. Rented videos were widely used in training to give the teacher a break in a long day; it didn't matter how long the programme is because the audience was captive anyhow. Comic videos provided light relief; providing they were relevant they helped kick off the session or wake up the group in the graveyard session after lunch.

In human resource development, on the other hand, sophisticated communicators used video very differently. They tended to edit programmes down to short sequences. They built their own package around these sequences. Importantly, they used these short sequences as a means of stimulating debate or even to quiz their group. Many others, however, didn't use video at all.

Whether through study of the principles of learning theory or through an intuitive grasp of effective practice, these HRD specialists are designing their programmes in ways which accord with the best demonstrated paradigms of cognitive psychology. George Miller suggested that most human beings cannot recall, process, act on or retain more items or issues than the magic number seven, plus or minus two, without considerable practice. Most environments within which corporate communications are delivered are ill adapted for best results. In these circumstances, the human attention span is generally limited to a few minutes on any topic and the number of key concepts that can be effectively acquired in a single session, no matter how well a communication is designed, is probably rather less than the magic number seven.

There are also a number of other key psychological concepts which are worthy of consideration and are borne out by the research. The psychologist Cherry adapted the principles of mathematical information theory, which analyses machine to machine transmissions, to the study of human communications. While much of the theory is too mechanical for the complexities of human interaction one concept, that of redundancy, proved to be important. Not everybody receives information best in the same way. Sometimes people may miss an essential idea or message if it is only expressed in one form. Therefore it is often valuable to express key components of a message in more than one medium. HRD experts often do this by reinforcement of a message on video, in text and through discussion.

Short sessions of any one medium are more effective because they maximise the primacy and recency effects. Research shows that individuals remember information at the beginning and end of sequences to a far greater degree than that in the middle. The longer a sequence, the less the information in the middle is likely to be retained. Short, sharp sequences are most effective.

These findings led Workhouse to change radically the product we offer our clients. We introduced desktop publishing to enable us to produce text materials, we recruited a number of experienced trainers and communicators, notably Dr Aldwyn Cooper who is one of the authors of this book, and we rethought the design of our video product.

The new approach was built on this Quadrangle finding. Old videos grew out of the teaching process. New videos must grow out of the learning process, based on an understanding of the part which media can play in stimulating discussion and ownership. Above all, we learned to understand the importance of engaging the attention of the participants rather than allowing them to view with their brains in neutral.

There's little new about this approach – it has been used in classrooms since time immemorial – 'Listen, because I'll be asking questions afterwards.' We were asked by Nomura International to persuade indifferent bankers to use assessment interview techniques – about which they knew nothing and cared less. We constructed a series of drama scenes which challenged the audience to spot precisely what was wrong, or right, about the conduct of these interviews and tell the facilitator at the end of each sequence. When Rover needed to demonstrate to its workers the rationale behind its new 'just in times' programme our 'trigger' consisted of an illuminating account of the horrors involved when the company built first, sold later; the new regime was successfully introduced and Rover's fortunes changed dramatically.

Price Waterhouse chose a pretty blunt method of provoking its partners to adopt a new attitude towards their managerial responsibilities; an outside firm had conducted a study that compared the way in which its clients regarded the firm with the partners' own perception; the partners were confronted with an eye-opening account of the mismatch between the two and invited to discuss the remedy.

The three cases above all use the motivational effect of

reducing 'cognitive dissonance' in the audience. Cognitive dissonance exists within an individual when there is an imbalance between an observed or experienced situation and the attitudes held and behaviours normally carried out by that individual. Dissonance is uncomfortable and people seek to reduce it by any means possible. In everyday life this is often achieved by negating or denying some aspects of the situation or by rationalising and reinterpreting dissonant information. The communications exercise at Price Waterhouse forced partners to confront the dissonance between their comfortable perceptions of clients' views and reality. This created a high level of motivation for the partners to adopt new behaviours and attitudes to reduce the distressing cognitive dissonance. It worked well.

It is now a truism that communication has to take place in both directions, allowing the workforce to contribute to the debate and encouraging them to play an active role in implementing the company's policy. On the wider canvas, this involves feedback loops, milestones, upwards appraisal and personal action plans – the armoury of today's professional communications manager.

Once more, the importance of these activities is backed up by psychological research. Earlier in the chapter we mentioned the Hawthorne study which demonstrated the importance of motivating staff through their feeling of involvement. There are two other principles which are of importance here. The first shows how carrying out activities and being forced to process information substantially improves retention, sometimes described as the effort theory of learning. It is, of course, easy to see why this might be true. Carrying out an exercise around a topic forces one to review it in a number of ways increasing the rehearsal of the content and also the range of associations both of which have been shown to be essential factors in strengthening memory.

The second is an interesting phenomenon termed the 'Zeigarnik effect'. It has been shown that individuals retain a far higher degree of memory about a topic while they are still engaged in a task in which it is directly involved. While the task is being carried out there is obviously a high degree of motivation to remember facts and issues. Zeigarnik himself called this the 'tension' to remember something until it is finished. At that point, no matter how well information was originally known or rehearsed, the tension is lost and memory starts to decay. Therefore, maintaining activity with personal plans, feedback loops and continuing exercises refreshes the memory through almost unconscious rehearsal. Focusing down, as we did, on the design of the small-arms in the communications war, we discovered that bullets and triggers are more effective than missiles and barrages – triggers which provoke discussion, bullet points which drive home the message.

One of the research studies – the Business Research Unit's study on behalf of the CBI – helped to refine this approach by providing invaluable advice as to the form in which senior executives feel that their information should be packaged. The CBI wanted to communicate an important message to people whom it knew to be busy, impatient of wasted time and who demand quality and effectiveness. Chief executives were questioned about the different media of communications, not only which medium they preferred but in what form they preferred it.

The survey demonstrated that the CEO doesn't want precious time wasted with flabby verbose messages, or with generic material which doesn't apply to his or her own company's situation, or which is out of date. It established that the CEO is a surprisingly isolated creature who wants to see how other firms perform and other chief executives behave. Reassuringly for us, the bosses clearly preferred video over other media because it saves valuable time. The techniques of interviewing and editing which video has inherited from television help select only the most important information and to compress the message. Eight or ten minutes watching and hearing a video conveyed more information than twice that of time spent reading or listening.

The CEOs were also surprisingly discriminating in their

viewing. Analysis showed that they disliked programmes presented by TV personalities pretending to speak for a company, preferring to hear from other business people or academics with genuine knowledge of commerce and industry, they hated any clash between pictures and commentary, especially when graphics were on the screen, they were picky about the use of music and they loathed any suggestion of hype in the commentary. In short, they demand Gucci television: crisp, relevant, stylish.

Of course, Chief Executives may well be a breed apart in many ways. However, they do reflect the same perspectives on media as their workforces. The research has shown that one of the most important parts of planning a corporate communications programme is in tailoring the media and the messages to the different layers within the organisation and in attempting to avoid the major barriers to effective communication. These can be identified as:

- unstated assumptions
- receiver capacity
- incompatibility of cognitive schemas
- confused presentation
- distraction/noise/interference.

Unstated assumptions

Perhaps the most common fault in designing communications is for the designer to make an assumption about commonly held values or facts without making this explicit. It is all too easy for managers to assume that background information, plans, or terminology which are everyday knowledge to them are shared with all employees. This can either lead to blank incomprehension or to misinterpretation. However, research has also shown that communications should not be reduced to the lowest common denominator. Flat simplistic communication reduces motivation and loses effect.

Receiver capacity

Human beings are complex information processing channels. While they are not able to pay full attention to more than one source of information at a time they are able to switch rapidly from one to another. The tendency of the human receiver is to impose meaning on any material gathered and this serves to extend the amount of information that can be handled. Therefore, partial information gleaned from a variety of sources can often be re-assembled into a number of different, complete and almost accurate messages.

The capacity to assemble and retain meaningful messages is dependent on the existing knowledge base and on expectation. This is why materials or activities which provide background knowledge or orient the receiver are so valuable before any 'mass' communications are carried out. Communicators should analyse the background knowledge and expectation of the audience in detail before designing the communications package. However, once the channels become genuinely overloaded, reception and interpretation become rapidly lost. Try to limit the number of major concepts to the lower bands of George Miller's 'Magic number seven plus or minus two' and try to maintain an adequate level of 'redundancy' to substitute for any information lost through processor capacity limitation.

Incompatibility of cognitive schemas

This rather high-flown term has a simple and important meaning. Every individual has his or her own ways of interpreting the world, based on their own experiences. These 'schemas' are established over long periods of time and tend to be well established. They tend to control the way that people think, believe, talk and behave. Any communication that is received is compared against the individual's own schema for interpretation and action. If the information is expressed imprecisely it can lead to an interpretation substantially different from the intended message. If the communication does not match the individual's schema at all, it is likely to be completely rejected, for example, top television presenters featured in videos and apparently claiming knowledge of companies in which they have never had any involvement. Such programmes have no credibility. There are numerous examples of failed employee communications programmes where the content of the message from senior management on the top floor does not match the schemas of the employees derived from experience on the shop floor. Communications managers should maintain a regularly updated, stated definition of the most widely held beliefs and schemas of their audiences. This will entail regular attitude and in-depth awareness surveys.

Confused presentation

It may seem like a truism but it is quite clear from the research that it is possible to include all the essential meaning in a message but to destroy its intelligibility by failing to pay attention to the details of presentation. In the end it is the final details that often decide whether a communication is effective or not and it is often this aspect of development that receives least attention.

There are so many issues which can effect the results. These can range from the ordering of the main points in the message through the language used to the examples used for illustration. Research in human memory has shown that careful attention to the ordering of issues and ideas makes considerable difference to retention of information. Associative memory studies show that the guiding characteristic is not necessarily a flow of logic but rather the associations between different concepts that have grown up out of use. Developing an associative chain within the communication can have more impact than honing logic and detail.

There are also different concerns for different media. In text, for example, line length, font style, page size, proportion of blank space to text, paper quality and many other character-istics can have radical effects. There are some obvious guide-lines such as: text must be readable in average light conditions; do not use line lengths longer than can be scanned in one pass; maintain a consistent style for denoting section structure or weighting, or use colour for carefully selected emphasis and avoid colours which interfere with each other. However, others are less intuitive. For some audiences, densely packed text is more effective than well-spaced designs because the receivers associate the latter with simplistic concepts, not worth their attention. Inappropriate paper quality, too expensive or too crude, may not match to the audiences' expectations or the nature of the message which is being presented. Careful attention to this kind of detail can substantially improve reception and understanding of text.

In video it can be the type of camera work, the quality of the shot, the graphics, the music or the presenter which can make the difference between success and failure. In audio, tone of voice, tempo, phrasing and music all play their role. There are no simple rules and a thorough analysis of the audience and corporate culture is essential. For example, some organisations have found recently that video produced inexpensively by the staff themselves using hand-held camcorder equipment is far more effective in conveying some types of message than carefully scripted and produced corporate productions costing ten times as much. Others, who have tried to jump on this bandwagon for reasons of cost saving, have found that in-appropriate use of this informal type of approach can destroy credibility of management in the eyes of the workforce that, long-term, costs far more than adopting a high-quality pro-fessional approach from the outset.

Distraction/noise/interference

There are essentially three different sets of stimuli which can interfere with communications: competing stimuli, environmental factors and internal stress. It may seem clear that noise or distractions while a communication is taking place are likely to interfere with understanding. However, it is possible that the absence of competing stimuli can also have a negative effect. In some situations, the activities taking place around the communications can have the effect of locking the message into memory through establishing the communication as part of normal experience rather than as something alien and different which may cause debilitating stress. Further, experiments have shown that the nature of the activities before and after a communications session can have just as much effect on comprehension or retention. It is quite possible to ruin the effect of a perfect communications session by organising follow-up activities which are diversionary.

It might be thought that a calm environment with comfortable seating and well-maintained temperature humidity etc would be ideal. However, such a situation may be disconcertingly different from the normal working environment and may create tensions once more. It has also been shown that certain levels of discomfort can heighten awareness and reinforce effectiveness. Each situation needs careful analysis.

Internal stress can be of a variety of types in both the communicator and the audience. It can be stress brought on by personal factors such as illness, tiredness, depression or personal circumstances or amplified by group concerns. While it is usually impossible to understand the individual concerns of each member of the audience, structuring the communication around an awareness of group tensions can be used to strengthen retention of messages.

For communicators themselves, there are two other sources of stress. The most obvious is caused by the communicator's lack of familiarity with the media or personal belief. It is still assumed all too often that managers must be able to speak in public, use overhead slides, videos, audios and lead group discussions without training. The second is where the communicator's own values and beliefs are at variance with the ideas that they are being asked to present. Many cascade communications exercises have foundered on the rock of communicator incompetence and the subtle adjustment to audience perception that can be caused by the body language of presenters who are uncomfortable with their messages.

Essential issues in communications are as complex as human cognition itself. None the less, there are a number of clear lessons that can be drawn from the research:

- The message will only be fully received if the audience is motivated, engaged, triggered and involved not just in theory but in hard specific measurable fact.
- People are cynical of presentations that seem to have been prepared for wider audiences and contain elements which are irrelevant to them or lack credibility.
- Although the message needs to be carefully designed by the relevant managers, the presentation of each element in the communications process needs to be defined carefully to meet the needs and expectations of the intended audience rather than the preferences of the communicator.
- The delivery channel and location for the communication needs to be carefully selected to ensure that it will reach the highest possible proportion of the intended audience in ways which they will find motivating and where they will be able to pay attention to the message.
- The right media must be selected to perform the task which each medium performs best. Videos that attempt to communicate detailed information or text that tries to capture the enthusiasm of a charismatic communicator are less effective than, say, printed material or a public performance by the communicator in person.

This leads to the most important point of all. With today's technology and in the best of all possible circumstances, *The most effective form of communication is usually a face-to-face briefing. Media are best used to support the facilitator. But, conversely, the human being is only as good as his or her own communications skills, the briefing that he or she has been given and the demonstrable commitment of the company to listen to the views of the people who are taking part and to take relevant action.* But sometimes – a carefully prepared media pack can be the best solution.

3

Plot Your Route – AEA Technology, Price Waterhouse MCS

'Communications is the central nervous system of any organisation', says Kevin Murray. 'Unless it is fully integrated and controlled from one source, it cannot be effective'. Murray is Director of Communications at AEA Technology, an organisation which in the early 1990s achieved a near-permanent state of change, and the subject of our first case study. As it approached privatisation and a sea-change from its status as a government-owned agency, the medium virtually became the message, communication the leading edge of strategy.

The other case study in this chapter is an example of 'physician cure thyself'. Following a depressing period of re-organisation and recession, Price Waterhouse Management Consultancy Services (PW MCS) decided in 1993 that it needed to unify its partners and staff and give them a clear sense of direction. It set about the project with a sense of purpose and a well-defined route map – the very medicine it prescribes for its clients.

Each of these case studies is a model of its kind in that both companies laid the ground carefully before embarking on major communications. AEA Technology, as you will read, used research techniques to establish precisely what its clients thought of the company, and what its staff felt about the means it uses for communicating with them. PW MCS used the process of planning as the means for enlisting support from its partners, the very people whose discord and lack of focus was threatening to destroy the firm.

There are points of difference between the two studies. Kevin Murray is the very model of a modern communications manager; he has command of all the skills and resources needed for distributing information across a widespread work-force, his position within AEA Technology gives him both power and influence where it is needed, he has a clear job description and a philosophy for communication. PW MCS does not, on the other hand, have a clearly identified communications manager. It relied on the unstinting efforts of three people – the Director of the European firm, Peter Davis, the change management specialist, Clive Newton, and the marketing manager, Geoff Dodds. Between them they commanded the strategic and technical skills needed for the job; they also employed outside experts where they knew their own experience was deficient.

From the outset, both AEA Technology and PW MCS had clear strategies and plans; their communications teams had the full support of their leadership; they were familiar with the techniques to be used.

The importance of research

It has already been mentioned that each organisation started its programme with a comprehensive research study, AEA Technology focusing on the perceptions of its clients and potential clients, PW MCS on the attitudes of its staff. These surveys were significant triggers to the process of change, creating in both organisations the realisation that something had to be done.

PW MCS also used the research process to help bring all its partners into the fold. The firm has over a hundred partners, a form of industrial democracy which makes it hard to secure agreement for radical new strategies. By involving them all in focus groups, discussing the emerging strategy and feeding back the results of other such group debates, the firm's disparate leadership was brought gradually on board; then, when the time came to embed the strategy in media, the process of recording interviews had an additional effect in laying down a harmonised message publicly endorsed by the two-dozen most senior partners. Research had been the catalyst whereby the leadership came to 'sing from the same hymn sheet'.

Top dogs

Both case studies, too, demonstrate the importance of another factor which will recur throughout the book – the role of the man or woman at the top (alas – there are no women in this role in any of the case studies we report). Peter Davis of PW MCS took the best part of the summer of 1994 to present the new strategy personally to (almost) every member of the firm's 14,000 staff throughout Europe. As we shall see, Sir Anthony Cleaver of AEA Technology is a fully committed communicator who supports Kevin Murray every inch of the way.

AEA Technology – The medium is the message

There can be few more graphic illustrations of the power of communications to shape corporate strategy than the progress of Britain's Atomic Energy Authority from ivory tower to commercial street fighter. Formed in the 1950s it had symbolised the 'white heat of technology' bruited by Labour's young Technology Minister Tony Benn. In the days when nuclear energy had promised unlimited cheap energy, the organisation was run and operated by white-coated scientists and engineers. Harwell, Calder Hall, Risley, Windscale, its operations read like a roll-call of scientific endeavour in Britain. Chairmen of the United Kingdom Atomic Energy Authority (UKAEA), from William Penney to John Collier, were without exception distinguished practitioners of the nuclear field.

Then the tide turned against nuclear energy. Mishaps at Three Mile Island and Chernobyl rocked public opinion in Britain; the government responded by raising safety standards ever higher and with them the cost of operating nuclear stations and disposing of waste. As a result of mounting disquiet and doubtful profitability, it was announced in November 1989 that Britain's nuclear stations were to be withheld from the privatisation of the electricity supply industry and a moratorium was announced on building new reactors after Sizewell B. Nuclear Electric was formed and the whole nuclear industry was put on notice; its survival depended on its ability to show that it could stand on its own commercial feet. A Nuclear Review in 1994 was to place the whole sector under a magnifying glass, as we shall see in the case study of Nuclear Electric related in Chapter 6. The Review would also examine the role of the UKAEA.

Streetwise

The Authority's response to the government's gauntlet was to embark on a strenuous campaign to shed its quangoid culture. It was clear that the organisation had two distinct functions which fitted uneasily under the same roof (or rather roofs, since its people were spread throughout 13 different sites). On the one hand, the residual nuclear mission still held responsibility, on behalf of the government, for the safety, decommissioning and waste management of the UKAEA's nuclear plant. On the other hand, the self-styled commercial arm sold the scientific and engineering experience gained over 40 years of nuclear operation, and the expertise it had gained in helping optimise the performance of Britain's nuclear plants, especially safety techniques and protection of the environment. Techniques such as non-destructive testing, risk control and robotics developed initially in the construction, operation and decommissioning of nuclear stations, have proved to be of value to industries as varied as North Sea oil and aviation. This division would trade as AEA Technology under the umbrella of the UKAEA, known as the Authority.

In 1993 the Authority appointed a hard-headed businessman

as its first arts-educated chairman (Sir Anthony Cleaver had read Classics at Oxford before joining IBM, where he rose to Chairman and Chief Executive). Sir Anthony also has a clear commitment to communications. As Murray puts it, 'there was never any question what we were to communicate, just when and how. Cleaver is himself a brilliant communicator.'

Sir Anthony immediately ratified two important developments. Firstly, he accepted the conclusion that the two divisions required different management structures. Secondly, that the commercial arm, AEA Technology, could be privatised. The organisation was to be thrown into a period of massive change.

It couldn't have happened to a more demoralised and change-weary workforce. A newspaper described the UKAEA as 'Britain's brainiest organisation'. As Kevin Murray points out, scientists are by nature both challenging and cynical, and the UKAEA is more cynical than most. Staff were already shaken by a massive reduction in numbers – from 15,000 in 1988 to 7,000 in 1994. People who had started careers which offered a job for life now faced the hire-and-fire culture of private-sector management. Scientists whose motivation was pure R&D and who disdained profits would have to learn about bottom lines and return on investment.

The new broom

Kevin Murray had joined the UKAEA in April 1992, 15 months before the new Chairman. In terms of the research reported in Chapter 2, he fits firmly in the tradition of external relations – he is familiar with all the media and techniques involved in communication. However, having been head-hunted to fill a purely public relations role, Murray made it clear that he was only interested if he had complete control of the whole communications process, internal and external.

Murray recognised that privatisation was a possible route forward for the Authority; he believed he could best help this come about if the function were integrated 'not just across PR, direct mail etc but across every one of the audiences'. His job description states that one of his targets is 'to help the organisation clarify and achieve corporate objectives through good communications'.

Murray knew that before he could formulate a communications strategy he needed adequate information. This led him to commission the first in a number of research studies which were to characterise his approach to the task in hand. For this first survey, he didn't use one of the large audit companies he was to employ later, to assess and analyse quantitative data. Instead, he called on Stuart Hyslop Editorial Services, a niche bureau run by an ex-Fleet Street journalist. This was a qualitative study in which two hundred people were interviewed across the company's audiences, external and internal.

Hyslop provided his own commentary on the findings of his survey, and his first question to Murray was blunt: 'Did you know what you were taking on when you accepted this job?' To all intents and purposes, the Authority was in a mess.

The company was operating as a number of 'cottage industries'. Every business appeared to have its own marketing and sales units which flew in the face of the fact that the company's future lay in integrated contracts with blue-chip companies. The image was hopelessly fragmented, 'to the point of schizophrenia' says Murray.

On the other side of the coin, AEA Technology's management had still to appreciate what they had let themselves in for with their new Director of Communications. They had expected Murray to follow his predecessors and act as the public spokesperson for the organisation. In fact, he did the opposite. He made them do the talking whilst he saw his own role as that of consultant and strategist. Murray operates a policy of 'universal prescription, local dose' – the managers know their own patch and they should appear in public talking about subjects in which they are expert. They should sing, however, from a hymn sheet written and orchestrated by the Communications division.

Inevitably, the maestro had strong views concerning the type of music his managers should sing. For instance, he abhors press conferences; instead, at times of important announcements, he 'chains the chairman to his desk' and lines up a series of telephone interviews with selected journalists. His role was less that of mouthpiece, more as strategist, not just for communications but for the organisation as a whole.

As a result of the Hyslop survey, Murray reported to the board that three key steps were needed. Firstly, the company had to articulate its vision of what it wanted to be. Its clients still thought of it as the R&D arm of the nuclear industry and were unaware of its attempt to position itself as a provider of scientific services to a broad range of clients. Secondly, it should have a new corporate identity. Thirdly, it should promote itself to the outside world – it had conducted virtually no advertising. He immediately applied for and won a 300 per cent increase in the advertising budget.

Although Murray was not the marketing director, the surveys he commissioned in the market-place highlighted clear messages for communicating the company's marketing policy; he recommended that the company focus its marketing efforts towards the sectors it served – articulating, for instance, 'the AEA's offer to the Chemicals Industry' . . . or defence, or oil exploration, sweeping up into that message the services of all relevant divisions.

Corporate identity

Above all, any message sent out to the market-place should be prepared in concert with the other messages the company was transmitting. The main vehicle through which this new unity would be conveyed was to be a new corporate identity designed by Lloyd Northover.

The company, which had recently overhauled British Aerospace's livery, now produced another sleek design which was to be reflected in every crevice of AEA Technology. Lloyd Northover had been asked to research the proposed design among 40 of AEA Technology's customers; the survey had shown that people regarded the logo as 'dynamic, secure and friendly'. Straight lines in the heart of the logo were rendered curvy, and the research panel declared these to be 'environmental':

The theory was that the different units would all cluster together under a single brand image. The fact was that the rogue elements were far from ready to be enlisted. Knowing that he had a fight on his hands if he was to win the support of the whole company, Murray set up a corporate identity working party with representatives from each division; this group helped decide the final design and planned its introduction.

Every member of staff then received a direct mailshot and he personally conducted a travelling roadshow through which more than 600 managers were introduced to the concept. To ensure that performance was measured in both directions, a questionnaire was issued offering staff the opportunity to mark Kevin Murray's own performance.

Each of Murray's roadshow seminars started with a single slide showing a range of the literature which the company was at that time sending out to clients and external audiences. It showed a horrendous mixture of typefaces, colours and layouts – evidence that the company totally lacked direction and cohesion. He then showed the framework within which they were now to operate – once again, universal prescription, local dose. Even internal memoranda would carry the new logo –

the change affected every secretary, sales team, requisitions clerk and member of the board. They were free to tailor their designs within the rules, with the Corporate Communications Service making only spot checks on compliance.

The new design was reflected in two important communication campaigns. Externally, an advertising campaign was conducted based around the word Eureka. Internally, the house journal was re-designed with a new title. Both were built on a firm foundation of research findings. Research had showed that clients regarded the company as highly skilled in problem solving – the Eureka lightbulb symbol highlighted that. Names of non-nuclear clients indicated that AEA Technology had now diversified its service.

Measurement

Measurement lies at the heart of Murray's communications strategy – he describes himself as a research junkie. The company's employees are predominantly scientists for whom statistics are meat and drink. They were reassured by the data produced by a number of surveys, demonstrating that Murray's communications strategy was beginning to pay off.

One of the largest studies was conducted by MORI in December 1993; it covered 200 companies, approximately 40 per cent of them existing and the other 60 per cent potential clients of the company. The Eureka campaign was followed by another survey, this time a quantitative study by MORI.

The results were impressive – awareness of AEA Technology had grown by 80 per cent whilst fully 75 per cent of those surveyed reckoned it was 'the kind of organisation we'd like to work with'. Eighty per cent regarded AEA Technology as 'good at solving scientific and engineering problems' – the very goal it had set itself in the commercial marketplace. On the negative side, outsiders regarded the staff of AEA Technology as still imbued with civil service attitudes and were not happy with the company's commercial procedures for tendering, invoicing, contracting and so on.

Murray commissioned a further survey from MORI to test attitudes to AEA Technology among the research firm's 'captains of industry' panel. Again, the results were favourable – in 1991 only 40 per cent of these leading figures had heard of AEA Technology; in 1994 that figure had risen to 55 per cent and the 1994 research further demonstrated that the company's clients now believed that it understands the markets it is serving. Even the 'civil service' attitudes of the staff were seen slowly to be changing.

Altogether, Murray has commissioned over a dozen surveys in the two-and-a-half year period during which he has been Director of Communications at the Authority, and he is still going strong. The new identity of the house journal was also measured. It out-performed its predecessors in all the important criteria – 'Keeps me up to date', 'Is interesting to read', 'Helps me feel part of AEA', 'Gives a balanced view'. Interestingly, the number of people who felt that it 'only gives the management view' had declined from 64 per cent to 44 per cent.

Every edition of the *AEA Times* carries questionnaires for its readers to complete and attitudes are further tested by focus panels which provide qualitative feedback on attitudes to the journal and to the organisation. The staff's own verdict was confirmed by communications professionals – in the same year, the new *AEA Times* immediately won outright the award for the toughest and largest region in the British Association of Industrial Editors' employee newspaper awards – beating off such rivals as National Grid and Courtaulds.

By now, the Corporate Communication Service was a unit to be reckoned with. It had grown to 65 people, with a full range of services – print, photographic, video, design and so on.

The next advertising campaign was based on a Newton's cradle executive toy, with each ball imprinted with one of the services offered by AEA Technology – Product, Plant, Process, Safety, Environment. The purpose here was to articulate the proposition that the company brings integrated solutions to problems by bringing teams together. The agency's proposal suggested that companies would suffer from a knock-on effect should any stage be wrongly tackled – if the plant goes wrong it affects the process, then safety suffers, followed by environmental effects. 'You can't see the complete solution unless you understand the whole process.'

Restructuring

By mid-1994 the new Chairman was firmly in the saddle, and Sir Anthony had taken note of the findings from the various research studies which had been conducted by the Corporate Communications Service. He had now set clear strategies for the immediate future. The Authority would now become a holding company comprising the Board and nothing else. The rest was to be divided into two.

The Government division was to establish itself as the Agency to handle the Authority's public responsibilities – safety, waste disposal, decommissioning – firstly for the AEA's own plant and equipment and in time for other nuclear bodies. This division employs 1,900 people and turns over £200 million. This step would immediately ease the route towards privatising AEA Technology, the Commercial division, by providing the government with a formula under which it could split off those activities which the financial world doesn't fully understand or trust. When the government agreed to the privatisation of Nuclear Electric, the same formula could apply: the AEA's Government division could take over responsibility for decommissioning and waste disposal for its reactors as well. The title of Nuclear Decommissioning Agency has been mooted for the Government division.

The Commercial division – AEA Technology – employs 4,000 people. The Queen's Speech in November 1994 finally cleared the path for it to be privatised – announcing that there would be a Bill in the next Parliament following further discussions on the precise form and content it should take. The division's turnover of £250 million in 1993/94 was built on the company's traditional prowess in securing both public sector business from its traditional partner and sales to the rest of industry as well as to governments around the world. There was an urgency to secure new work; in 1993/94 the decline of traditional business had been sufficiently serious to wipe out the effect of increases in British private sector work of 30 per cent in that year and in overseas work of 40 per cent.

Whilst the operating divisions were split in two, the Central Services – including Communications – were themselves undergoing reorganisation. At first, Central Services continued as a single, separate entity servicing both the new companies. Then, in August 1994, parts of this unit were split off and absorbed into the Government or Commercial divisions. The remaining infrastructure was consolidated into a new Facilities Services division FSD, responsible for managing the Authority's facilities. The plan was to sell off the FSD with a year's worth of guaranteed contracts worth £100 million.

The latest changes produced a fresh spate of agony. People who had worked alongside each other were now placed in increasingly adversarial positions. Public service procurement policies required the Government division to throw open all its contracts to competition among external providers, of which the Commercial division was now just one among many. The FSD was obliged to secure the best terms possible for providing buildings and facilities to the other two; internal rents, site engineering contracts, canteen prices and the rest had now to be rigidly negotiated so that each unit could demonstrate its own profitability – which each needed to do if it was to present an attractive prospect for potential backers or purchasers. Whilst the Authority had applied the rules of the 'internal market' to the three divisions, the staff had inevitably found it easier to deal with their colleagues than with outsiders. Now, the cosy flow of work from one division to the other was to be replaced by tough external negotiations and professional purchasing techniques.

Murray himself moved to AEA Technology, the Commercial division, where he became a member of the Management Committee, while still reporting directly to the Chairman and Chief Executive of the Authority on Group Affairs.

Communicating change

As the torrent of change continued unabated, AEA Technology still developed fresh techniques for keeping staff informed. An Internal Communications Action Plan was prepared, on the back of yet another MORI poll, this time of employee attitudes. The plan was designed to ensure that the company's vision was cascaded throughout the organisation; each person's specific role was explained to him or her. A series of roadshows kept managers in touch with developments; again, nothing was left to guesswork. A member of the Communications team attended each roadshow, questionnaires were issued and the results fed back to the management.

Three thousand people in the company had direct access to a closed-circuit e-mail bulletin. If messages needed to reach more people as quickly as possible, a Facts Fax system, backed up by e-mail, carried the message with clear instructions to managers detailing what steps they needed to take to communicate further down the chain.

There are still weaknesses in the system. Murray believes that cascades would not yet work in AEA Technology because managers still lack the necessary skills. Training in communications techniques is being developed for those who find themselves ill at ease with difficult issues or who are observed to be poor listeners. Important messages are disseminated through printed leaflets, often issued as a supplement to the house journal.

To give the managers a role in the exercise, they are instructed to hold feedback sessions asking staff for their reactions to the content of the message, and they are obliged to report the findings. Even this process has unexpected results –

one unit reported that they didn't previously know of the existence of the manager who ran their group!

The feedback is reported in *AEA Times* and the Management Committee is briefed on the questions posed at the roadshows. When there are breakdowns, they are investigated. One team's briefing consisted of the manager reading the text of the message in a lifeless monotone and abruptly leaving; inevitably, the staff were dismayed and rumours began to fly. It emerged that the briefing had been poorly planned; the team's real manager was abroad at the time and the session need not have been arranged during his absence.

The bottom line

Every communications activity, external or internal, has been set clear objectives and meticulously measured against them. Murray applies the rule of 'One what and five why's' – what we are going to achieve and five reasons for doing so. Measurement criteria vary; most often they are defined in business terms – changes in behaviour leading to an improvement in the bottom line, achieving the positive or avoiding the negative. Sometimes, the cost of *not* communicating is a more important factor than the benefits of doing so.

The future

This book goes to press at a time when the future for AEA Technology is still unclear. It holds, if anything, more of a challenge than the turbulent period before Murray joined the UKAEA. On the one hand, the route towards privatisation and flotation is still subject to the vagaries of both government and market whim. Internally, on the other hand, the process of reorganisation goes on. PA Consultants were retained to conduct a business process re-engineering project on AEA Technology; Kevin Murray is joint project manager of the

project. Its recommendations will be implemented at the very
time when privatisation would be gathering a full head of
steam. The company needs by then to be able to demonstrate
increased profitability. Murray himself describes the pace of
change as breathtaking.

Taking stock

AEA Technology has turned attitude research into a managerial discipline – not every organisation can afford to and most do
not need to conduct as many surveys as this company *en route*
to partial privatisation. However, most organisations need to
conduct or commission some research into the perceptions
either of their staff or their clients, or both. Indeed, it is
depressing to note how few have done so.

Research doesn't simply reveal the attitudes of people to the
organisation – properly conducted, it conveys a number of
important messages in its own right. For one thing, it informs
the people taking part in the survey that someone, somewhere
is interested in what they think. When the survey is complete
and they see change resulting from it – as happened as a
consequence of Price Waterhouse's research – they are grati-
fied that the leadership has chosen to act in this way.

Another by-product of research can be to test assumptions
at senior level. A dozen people can leave a meeting each
convinced that there is unanimous agreement with the conclusions. When quizzed by an outsider, it often becomes clear that
they are harbouring a dozen different perceptions of what was
actually discussed and agreed.

It is possible for companies to conduct their own surveys –
up to a point. It can be cost-effective to hire a specialist agency
to design the formats to be used in the research, then to
conduct the legwork using internal resources. This book can do
no more than offer broad guidance to the DIY auditor;

however, for those brave, or poor enough to wish to conduct their own studies, here are a few pointers.

Firstly, it is essential to decide precisely what sort of information is needed. This may sound trite, but correct analysis is essential. For starters, are statistics required, or insights? The organisation may need information about the readership of the company newsletter, for example, or attitudes towards its content and style. It may want to assess how far the company's messages manage to penetrate through 'the system'. Where statistical information is needed concerning the behaviour and attitudes of a comparatively large proportion of the workforce a questionnaire is usually the most effective form of measurement.

In other cases, it is more important to explore more deeply the reasons which lie behind the attitudes, to add colour to the data which emerged from the quantitative survey, to test new ideas or policies. These call for qualitative research, usually involving a much smaller sample of the workforce, typically in a focus group or groups.

Groups should be led by a skilled facilitator and should ideally comprise no more than eight or ten people. The facilitator needs to be familiar with the company and to avoid becoming personally involved in the discussion; he or she is there to move the discussion along but, more importantly, to observe the pattern of information which emerges, to ignore the extreme and to encourage the reticent, to achieve a homogeneity of opinion across the different discussions and to record the findings.

A variation on group discussions is the one-to-one interview usually with senior members of the management team. An outsider who consistently asks direct, simple questions can unearth discord or misunderstandings among management teams; alternatively, as we shall again see from the Price Waterhouse case study, this technique can help reinforce harmony.

Each of the techniques offers a different perspective upon the attitudes of the workforce of a company or of its market.

Whichever format is chosen, success depends on the formulation of the questions. The multiple choices of the questionnaire will only yield valuable results if the questions are clearly stated, the choices are genuine and distinct and above all unbiased. One advantage of the printed form lies in the fact that respondents can be offered complete confidentiality; if guaranteed, it should be scrupulously observed.

Questionnaires can prove less useful if care isn't given to the choice of the sample which will be tested; too few can obviously be unrepresentative whilst, interestingly, the statisticians tell us that it adds little to the value of the findings if the sample is larger than 1,000 in number.

One advantage of questionnaires is that data can be easily collated. Assuming that the questions offer grades of response – from 'strongly agree' to 'strongly disagree', for example, 'excellent' to 'very bad', or from 'very often' to 'rarely' – which have values ranging from 0 to 5 or 6, then specialist computer bureaux can easily read and compile the results. These bureaux specialise in the design and formulation of questionnaires and it is sensible for the DIY research company to seek their advice in advance regarding the questions.

One golden rule for the cost-conscious company is to think carefully about the quantity and depth of information it really needs. Think hard about the samples who will be selected to take part, making sure that they represent the sectors of the workforce whose views are most valuable. Once you have started the process, stick with it. Kevin Murray's use of MORI polls shows how the results of earlier surveys can act as a bench-mark for later findings.

But beware; conducting surveys is like driving a car – a lot harder to perform than it looks, with potentially disastrous results when attempted by the totally inexperienced. The first rule is – it is important to establish just how your target audience really does receive information about the company. The second is – do it professionally. Price Waterhouse did, as the next case study will report.

Price Waterhouse Management Consultancy Services – Consultant heal thyself

'People didn't criticise the leadership, they simply didn't see any.' These words came from a young but rapidly rising PW MCS partner and they raised a laugh every time the video was played. MCS is the consultancy arm of Price Waterhouse (PW), one of the smallest (but none the less highly visible) of the Big Six accountancy firms.

Smallest, because unlike most of its large rivals Price Waterhouse avoided the rash of megamergers which brought Young together with Ernst, Coopers into Deloittes and transformed Peat Marwick Mitchell into the more cumbersomely named KPMG Peat Marwick. Arthur Andersen was the only other firm to remain on the shelf; even on its own, however, Arthur Andersen remains the largest accountancy and consultancy firm in the world. Highly visible, in that Price Waterhouse concentrates on blue-chip accounts, and with high stakes comes publicity.

In the late 1980s, PW had formed an umbrella organisation – Price Waterhouse Europe – to acknowledge the importance of integration across both the UK and the continent. It subsequently performed a number of mergers with smaller firms in continental Europe. This commendably 'communitaire' move was hampered for a time by a tendency for national offices to concentrate on their own client lists, and particularly by a tendency for the powerful and profitable British practice to underestimate the contribution which could be made by its continental colleagues.

At the same time, PW expanded its management consulting business. This was the boom business of the 1980s, particularly for the large accountancy firms. The audit service provides the platform, an understanding of the client's business and a long-term relationship with the management; who better to provide advice on other areas of the business than the same firm's consultancy arm?

Like the rest of the Big Six, PW had a difficult start to the 1990s. The European recession forced clients to examine more closely their use of professional advisers; this resulted in over-capacity and a series of high-profile bankruptcies which in turn led to a number of actions for damages against auditors. None of the Big Six was unaffected.

The uncertainty was exacerbated by a fundamental change in the consultancy marketplace which caused PW MCS to re-examine its strategy for the 1990s. It decided to embark on a major change programme throughout its European operations.

Staking out the territory

When the consultancy arm commissioned an advertising agency, Ogilvy and Mather, to conduct a communications strategy to increase awareness of the consultancy service, O&M responded with the frank suggestion that before PW MCS spent money on advertising it should decide precisely what message it wished to present to the world. In other words, it should establish its own identity.

To its credit, PW MCS understood the irony of the situation. Whilst its consultants were paid considerable sums of money to produce rabbits out of corporate hats by diagnosing faults in client companies, PW MCS had never applied the same diagnostic skills to its own corporate body. Also to its credit, the change management programme which followed was a model of its kind.

By this time, PW MCS had resolved one of the tensions between the UK practice and the European firm. Peter Davis's position as European Director had sat uneasily beside that of the UK Managing Partner; he was now defined unambiguously as the boss of the UK practice within the European firm, dissolving any split loyalties which existed between national and European managements. Peter Davis took personal charge of the change process; in the autumn of 1993 he formed a Culture Change Group which comprised a European team of, as he put it, 'people who had a tomorrow'. The first step was an audit of attitudes amongst the firm's own staff.

This audit was based on a tried and tested questionnaire used by PW MCS for its own clients. Its acronym is ACT – Ability to Change and Transform. PW MCS stresses that its questionnaire was intended only as the basis for discussion by the management team. Its purpose was to provide them with enough evidence to enable them to take action. Questionnaires were distributed to all PW MCS staff throughout Europe in four languages, in autumn 1993. The staff were guaranteed anonymity – names were not required. Where they chose to add verbatim comments these were recorded.

Thanks to repeated reminders, the response rate was high – 65 per cent. The tiny Dutch office achieved a 100 per cent return; significantly, the highest response rate from any of the UK offices was lower than all but one of the continental offices. The overall findings demonstrated that morale was indeed low, notably in the UK.

Low morale is, of course relative – which is why benchmarking is important. The findings were one-third higher than the results of a comparable survey which PW MCS had conducted in a car manufacturing company, but 25 per cent lower than those of a survey in an insurance company. Highly motivated consultants are, of course, inclined to cynicism but should none the less register much higher than both.

Attitudes to change were measured. The results showed that PW MCS was overwhelmingly in favour of change (only 19 per cent were opposed) but felt that the existing procedures prevent change taking place. Only 32 per cent disagreed with the suggestion that 'our culture is resistant to change'.

Staff saw their colleagues and themselves as willing to do more than the job required, but felt that their efforts went unrecognised. They felt they were reasonably well directed at individual levels, but poorly co-ordinated between units. Another barrier to co-operation and efficiency, as they saw it, was the firm's inadequate investment in technology and support systems. There were criticisms of the amount of time spent on internal procedures, and the lack of incentive to provide customer service.

And so it went on. The firm's commitment to training and personal development appeared to have all but disappeared during the recession years; in particular, consultants did not pass on the lessons learned on one account to consultants working with new clients on similar projects. Where it did succeed (and there had been no mass migration of clients away from PW!) success was seen to have been due to people circumventing the system rather than utilising it.

On the positive side, people felt challenged by their work and proud to be part of the PW organisation. The client list was seen to be exciting. Importantly, they felt able to speak their minds even when this meant disagreeing with their bosses. This coincided with a low opinion of management, who were seen to communicate too little, to be too busy to see their staff and to set no clear sense of direction. Like all surveys, the ACT questionnaire tended to accentuate the negative and to marginalise the positive (another reason for accurate bench-marking). Even after compensating for this factor, however, its findings were sobering in a highly paid, highly motivated firm which, at the end of the day, earned its fees by advising other firms on how to improve their performance.

Peter Davis now had enough evidence to act; the case for change was overwhelming. In December 1993 he invited the consultancy's Head of Organisational Change Management, Clive Newton, to lead one of the most intensive culture change programmes ever undertaken by a consultancy practice upon itself. Newton's aims were unequivocal: 'It is to be the best and most professional thing the firm has done. It must reach the most junior member of staff; we must be as good in talking to our own staff as we are in talking to clients; our recommendations to our own firm must be as good as our recommendations to outside companies.'

Following the audit, there were to be two main steps – defining the culture and communication. Defining the culture was primarily the task of the Culture Change Team and the framework of the ACT questionnaire provided the group with a shape on which to base their new 'target culture'. They drew up five headings:

- client service
- learning
- sharing
- challenging
- leadership.

The titles are, of course, all-embracing and bland. Controversy lurks, however, just below the surface. A firm dedicated to client service should make sure that its most effective partners devote their time to their customers – but surely it wants the best people inside the organisation to provide leadership and training? However much lip-service is paid to learning, it takes people out of commission whilst they are being trained and it distracts senior practitioners from their fee-paying work in order to spend time with their junior colleagues. Can a commitment to training be reconciled with the goal of dedication to client service?

If partners in different parts of Europe are to dedicate their time to sharing their expertise and efforts with colleagues in other offices or specialisms, how can they dedicate sufficient attention to their own clients? (This was aimed particularly at partners in the UK whose attitude to their continental colleagues had verged at times on the colonial.)

Challenging and leadership place the prestige of today's partners on the line as they are forced to encourage younger members of their team to question established practices and to act on their own initiative. The cauldron was well stocked with a brew of incendiary issues.

And so the list continues. By all accounts, the debates within the Culture Change Team were lively to the point of occasional acrimony, particularly when the most senior partners were challenged to show their dedication to client service by reducing some of their prestigious internal management roles. None

Figure 3.1
The Price Waterhouse culture wheel

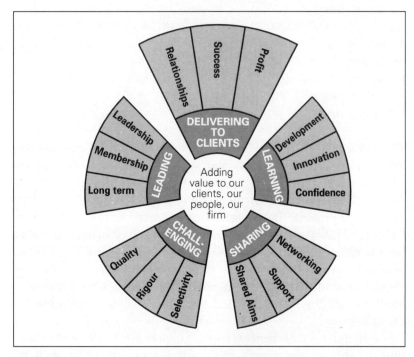

the less, the target culture emerged – a wheel with five segments reflecting the headings that had emerged from the questionnaire (see Figure 3.1). Each section was divided into three smaller segments and because client service was seen as the most important of the five, it was magnified above the others, giving it the appearance, to quote Peter Davis, of 'a cow-catcher at the front of a steam engine'. At the hub of the wheel sat the bullet point that feeds each of the spokes – 'Adding value to our clients, our people, our firms.'

Davis and Newton were all too aware that the most difficult obstacle to change lay in PW's constitution as a partnership. Every member of a partnership has, theoretically, an equal say in management issues, yet no organisation ever achieves clear objectives when real power is so broadly spread. As Peter

Davis put it, 'We had to get the partners on board or our work with the rest of the staff would be ruined by the actions of partners who were not following the new culture'. Clive Newton echoes this view, 'We had to get the partners on board and committed, so that they felt able to lead the business and be seen to be leading it. We approached this just like a client situation, engaging the partners to the target culture before anyone else heard about it.'

For this reason, they planned to start their campaign by persuading all partners that the target culture – the 'wheel' – was to represent the blueprint for the firm's shared values. Between February and April 1994, 20 workshops were held throughout Europe, involving every one of the consultancy's 130 partners, at which the draft culture was exposed to criticism and suggestion. A pattern emerged for these work-shops, described by Newton: 'The objective was to create an imperative for change. We did this by feeding back the results of the survey. They became aware that continuing as before was not an option. Then the group was presented with the draft of the culture and invited to wicket-roll that (ie smooth out the problems and knock it into shape).

'At later meetings we were able to feed back the recommen-dations of previous workshops, so that a pattern began to emerge. We had to get every group to the stage where they knew it was all or nothing; they couldn't cherry pick the target culture. *We* couldn't tell them what to decide, we had to ask but by doing that we turned their involvement into commit-ment and started the process whereby they took ownership.' The process was summarised in three short bullet points:

- understanding
- involvement
- buy-in.

The next stage was to be more complicated. Peter Davis had already undertaken to present the new culture in person to every one of the firm's offices around Europe – spread across

10 territories and 17 practice units with a concentration in the
UK, especially at the firm's London headquarters. It had long
been clear, however, that the most superhuman of communicators would have difficulty harnessing enthusiasm for the
culture within the bounds of a clear succinct explanation of its
content. Furthermore, it was important that staff be convinced
that all the senior partners were committed to change, and that
the firm was ready to dedicate sufficient resources to the
process.

The film of the book

To focus the target culture in a form which could be travelled
around Europe, to capture the enthusiasm of the firm's
leadership and to provide evidence that resources were being
dedicated to the process, it was agreed that Workhouse should
produce a series of video modules which would both demonstrate the change process and outline the target culture.

Even half an hour of highly condensed programming is not
enough to explain in detail each of the 15 spokes within the
culture wheel. It would in any case be undesirable to let the
video do all the work since it was important for staff to hear
their masters' voices and be able to ask them questions. The
video was to be part, but only part, of a series of presentations
fronted by Peter Davis who would be able to provide the
necessary detail and answer questions.

To show that the senior management of the firm was
unanimously signed up to the new target culture it was decided
that the video should place on view as many as possible of the
partners in charge of territories or disciplines so that staff could
see that they were all committed.

In the short time available, the only way to schedule the
interviews was to arrange filming in an antechamber to one or
other of the conference rooms where the intensive programme
of committee meetings was being held. PW MCS' marketing
manager Geoff Dodds was responsible for pulling them out

of the meeting, one by one, so that Michael Blakstad could interview them.

This arrangement had a similar effect as if the interviews had been held as part of a qualitative audit. The partners arrived for the interview session with their heads buzzing from the discussion which was going on in the other room; partner after partner recorded enthusiastic and articulate endorsements of the target culture. (When it came to editing their contribution, the main problem for the producers lay in deciding which of the many powerful statements to omit.) The video 'captured' the views of individual partners and placed them firmly on the record. Partners who might have been arguing the toss inside the committee room became strong supporters when the camera was turning. When their views were screened to wider audiences, they could no longer moderate or reverse their stated position, even if they wanted to! The result was a convincing display of unity and commitment, and of team-work.

In the first of the video sequences, partners and some staff were invited to state their criticisms of the practice and the reasons why change was needed. It takes a brave organisation to wash its soiled linen in public in this way, but none of the unscripted statements was diluted in any way during the editing process. 'Partners do not get involved in a lot of our client work; staff feel isolated at the coal face.' 'The firm is not providing enough technology support.' 'They didn't know what their future was.' These comments reflected closely the findings of the ACT survey.

The opening sequence of the video also visited the intensive work which had been invested in defining the target culture, by eavesdropping on the committee meetings whilst Clive Newton's voice-over described the lengthy process.

In each of a series of shorter sequences, the senior partners took three bites at each segment of the culture – answering a series of questions drafted by Geoff Dodds. First, they were asked to define the culture, to say what the 'client culture' or 'sharing' or the other headings meant *in practice* in PW MCS.

Then they listed what they saw as the main obstacles to the achievement of the target quality. Finally, they were invited to describe the key steps needed to achieve the target culture.

Once again, honesty and criticism were allowed to hold sway. Peter Davis in his interview stated that the main obstacles to a 'sharing' culture within PW MCS lay with the firm's UK partners – 'What we are trying to overcome is 2,000 years of history. The English working with the French, the French working with the Germans.'

Another senior partner criticised his colleagues for their tendency to build power bases within the firm rather than devote their time to client service. A support staff member stated, 'Like the cobbler's child is often the worst shod, the problem here is the firm's own staff get the least attention.'

In the final video module, the partners and staff were asked what would convince them that the firm meant business. 'Seeing the individuals who are talking about change actually change their behaviour,' said one manager. Each of the partners was asked the 'desert islands' question – 'If you could only have one of the five target segments, which would it be?' The rest of the partners were more or less equally divided between client service, learning, sharing and the rest but Peter Davis refused to choose – 'I want all of it, I want all of it, I want all of it.'

Brussels, June 1994

The videos were first screened to a meeting in Brussels of all PW MCS partners from throughout Europe – the essential first step if they were all to endorse the message. Peter Davis introduced an intensive morning session, followed by a 45-minute exposition by Clive Newton of the target culture, in which the six video modules were each followed by a brief explanation, with slides, of the meaning of each segment and of the implementation programme. In another session, video sequences were shown of PW MCS consultants working successfully with clients; these came from Germany (Braun Electronics), Brussels (Warner Lambert), Copenhagen (Unipost) and Paris (Rhone Poulenc). In the videos, clients were invited to comment on the value which they believed PW MCS had added.

These case studies were sliced into modules which followed the five headings of the culture, showing how client service, learning, sharing, challenging and leadership contributed to each of the accounts. There was a further session on the development of people and investment in technology, two important strategic areas which were to underpin the change programme.

The reaction of the partners was measured – as was the response to other sessions taking part at the Palais de Congres, where the rest of Price Waterhouse's European accountancy firm was in conference. To the delight of the culture change team the PW MCS presentation was voted, by some distance, the best of the sessions at what was by any standards a successful PW conference. More importantly, it was evident that the partners were now fully convinced that the culture wheel reflected the new direction the PW MCS practice should follow.

Some partners expressed surprise, even shock, at seeing the consultancy's leadership admitting that PW MCS lacked leadership, and at the degree of criticism they were prepared to level at their own achievements. That was a small price to pay, however, for the overwhelming response that 'You have cut through the double-dealing, the internal politics. You've expressed exactly what I feel, too.' There was special praise for Peter Davis' straight talking, and the event was rated a personal triumph for him.

Not surprisingly, Davis himself voted it 'the best MCS session ever'. He was particularly pleased that partners had said they were impressed by the honesty of the videos – and stressed the part played by the case study videos of client accounts throughout Europe in demonstrating how the target culture served to underpin best practice in serving clients.

The Change Management Team was now convinced that the first of its goals had been achieved – the firm's partners were now signed up to the target culture. Now came stage two, the roll-out to the rest of the staff of PW MCS, some 1,600 professionals.

Roll-out

Immediately after the Brussels screening it was debated whether the videos should be doctored for the wider audience, not specifically in order to tone down the criticisms but to reduce the level of communication for what would, out in the field, be shorter sessions and with less well-informed audiences. Bravely, it was decided that no changes should be made, which Davis reckoned left him with no option but to attend as many of the screenings as possible; 'The videos were too dangerous to be shown without me being there!' For those sessions which he was unable to attend, either the firm's second most senior partner, Mark Austen, or Clive Newton took Davis' place; Geoff Dodds attended them all as organiser and rapporteur. In July 1994, the show got on the road.

Today, Peter Davis describes the process as time-consuming but a pleasure when it went right – 'which it did in every office' – a rare claim.

He feels it would have been better to have translated the programmes into some of the continental languages; although English is the international language of consultancy – and in Germany, Belgium and Denmark, for instance, staff do speak it fluently – in more southern parts of the continent people tend to understand it less well. Wherever possible, a local member of the Culture Change Team presented the section which Newton had unveiled at Brussels, giving a detailed description of the contents of the culture wheel, tailored to the country in which the presentation was taking place.

Follow-through

There was no way in which these presentations could be genuinely interactive – the target culture could categorically not be subjected to fresh ideas and amended at this stage. Furthermore, Newton was aware that the firm had to confront its own weaknesses in managing a culture change: 'We are not yet professional in managing the dynamics, at securing genuine engagement and involvement.'

Davis adds another hurdle: 'At the outset there was a genuine crisis to provide momentum. The first reaction to the first phase of the programme was "it's hurting, so we are addressing the right issues". The problem is, where do we go from here? The whole programme will take up to three years, and the second year will be more difficult than the first simply because things are better now.'

In the autumn of 1994, PW MCS carried out a second survey of staff. Newton was determined that this, too, should be a highly professional exercise, a 12-page well-designed booklet with a glossy cover and questions posed in seven languages. The response rate was 64 per cent, the same as the first questionnaire but a more impressive statistic at a time when the business was evidently performing so much better than in the previous year; 90 per cent of the partners had responded, followed by 66 per cent of other fee-earning staff and over 50 per cent of support staff.

Morale was seen to have improved, with almost 60 per cent of people now disagreeing with the statement that 'my morale is low'. The same percentage believed that real progress was being made in improving the way the practice operated – a reflection of the real investment which had been made in technology support, with IT no longer on the list of concerns.

Davis is pleased that the UK appears from the survey to have been subsumed for the first time into the pan-European strategy: 'Although each country has responded differently, as is to be expected, the results show that there has been a change in behaviour and attitude right across the board. People seem to be aware that they must play to the European game plan.'

Equally important, commercial results reinforce the attitude survey. European sales were over 25 per cent up on the same period in the previous year and the net margin too was 25 per cent ahead of budget. The firm's strategy was to elevate itself from the rat race, in which up to 20 rivals are invited to tender for consultancies, to the premier league in which PW MCS would face only three or four competitors in each tender – a privilege only achievable if a significant proportion of its accounts were truly multinational. By the end of 1994, 25 per cent of the firm's business was 'networked' – involving two or more offices across Europe (up from just 10 per cent in 1993). Profitability had leapt ahead accordingly.

These broad-brush figures reinforce the nuts and bolts of the change strategy. The firm has a detailed implementation plan for the year ahead. It involves a number of minutiae – for instance, the agenda of every management meeting takes its headings from the spokes of the culture wheel. Every computer's screen saver carries an image of the wheel and there is a coloured copy of the wheel on every partner's office wall.

There have also been a number of what Newton calls 'hard-side' changes. The firm promised to provide every member of staff with a lap-top computer, to enable them to work as efficiently when on location visiting clients as they do in the office. PW is the world's largest user of Lotus Notes with an installed base of 40,000 – Newton describes this network as the largest driver of culture in the firm.

There were 'soft-side' changes as well. Peer ratings are to be reported at management meetings (only the positive aspects are mentioned). Upward feedback has been introduced, first by junior partners of their senior colleagues, then of supervisors and managers by their subordinates.

PW MCS committed itself to providing every member of staff with no fewer than 10 days' training a year. It has also succeeded in its undertaking to re-structure its businesses.

Tomorrow the world!

Davis and Newton are, however, all too well aware that there
is still much to do. They believe they have won the support of
the partners for the change programme; they have still to
ensure that the shared values are spread through every part of
the practice. This will involve continued reinforcement by
ever-larger numbers of people – too many to allow genuine
debate. As Clive Newton puts it, 'We have to break down the
status differential and strengthen the voice of the people.'
Peter Davis knows that he must himself step back sufficiently
to allow less senior people to implement the strategy, but not
so far that people question his commitment – perhaps the most
difficult judgement of all when the process has been so visibly
and vigorously led.

Newton believes firmly that change programmes 'hang on
physical events. Organisations are driven by events – you must
build your structure around them.' From now on, the firm will
hold six-monthly staff days, in groups of between 40 and 200
people. These will each be attended by a member of the
Executive and facilitated either by Newton himself or by
another change expert, Dick Watkins. They will survey the
results of activities to date and set an agenda for each practice
group. They will ask staff to suggest the changes which they,
individually, will make to support the culture. Again, the
objectives will echo those of the partner workshops – understanding, involvement, buy-in.

The goal is to engage fully every member of staff by the
summer of 1995 – quite a challenge when, as Newton points
out, the level of skill in communication varies so widely
between the different offices; 'Some have no idea of such basic
techniques as how much information to put on a single slide.'
For this reason, an ambitious coaching programme has been
introduced. It started with a three-day programme for selected
partners run by David Hemery, the veteran British Olympian.
In June each year, the partners will meet again at the annual

convention of all Price Waterhouse's European partners. Each year, in July, the firm will hold a staff day, the theme of which will be the improvement of quality of supervision. PW MCS is actively examining ways in which the new technologies of communication will make it possible to allow 16,000 staff to be involved in the process at their respective levels, to interact but not to muddy the message. The sails of change are hoisted; the danger is that the wind will die leaving the vessel calmed.

Postscript

The role of Peter Davis – and the dilemma he now faces – raise one of the principal issues which pervade this book, the role of the most senior executive in the communications process. In subsequent chapters we shall meet a number of chief executives/chairmen who imprinted their personalities firmly on the strategies for which they had been responsible, with varying degrees of success.

The boss should be seen to endorse the message enthusiastic-ally and articulately. Peter Davis, as we have seen, took it upon himself to present the Culture Wheel to as many PW MCS offices throughout Europe as he possibly could. Anita Roddick allocates half of all her time to visiting Body Shop branches throughout the world – she regards face-to-face meetings as the most important part of the chief executive's role.

Not every chief executive can allocate this proportion of his or her time to meeting their staff; in large, geographically widespread organisations the 'personal touch' is only practical by means of the medium – normally video – which places the boss's endorsement firmly on record for all to see.

Endorsement doesn't stop, however, with the recorded interview; the everyday behaviour of the senior executive is even more significant. Peter Davis was infamous for his habit of arriving late at meetings, a clear breach of the new culture. Embarrassed, he agreed to pay £10 on the spot to the chairman of any meeting at which he arrived late. He claims it has cost him a fortune, but the point was made.

There are other, more telling ways, in which the person responsible for the message can play a key role in its implementation. PW MCS has introduced upward appraisals, laying open the most senior figures to criticism by the people who refer to them.

The same kind of accountability should apply to the process of communication; if the chief executive listens to the feedback and insists on action being taken as a result, then word spreads throughout the organisation that someone up there is taking notice.

Tailoring the message

Too much democracy leads to anarchy. As we shall see, it is vital that people at every level in the organisation are invited to debate the issues and that their opinions are fed back to the leadership. If they aren't involved they will feel alienated from the policies.

This feedback would be a farce if no action was ever taken however salient the points which emerged. However, no company can implement its strategy if every paragraph is subject to endless amendments and revisions. In the early 1990s the BBC attempted to launch Producer Choice, a policy which effectively placed the Corporation's resource departments on the open market. Producers could now invite competitive tenders from both internal units and outside companies. It was decided that this radical strategy should be democratically debated, and a large number of working parties were established to debate the proposed policies.

Senior programme makers and managers were invited to dig up the grass to see how the roots were growing – every aspect of the BBC's activities were subject to deep and intelligent scrutiny. The proposals came flooding back, many of them radical and most of them well constructed. The problem was, there was no way that the Directorate could go back completely on its draft strategy.

The rule is, tailor involvement to the level of the strategy most relevant to the group in question. PW MCS demonstrated the value of exposing the target culture to intensive debate by all its partners; this was essential if the firm's 'owners' were to support the new philosophy. But it would have been fatal then to invite every consultant, manager and staff member to join in analysing every aspect of the whole culture wheel.

When PW MCS does roll out the full culture to the next layer of staff it will have identified a number of specific aspects within the overall philosophy which the consultants and managers should usefully debate, with an agenda for personal and group actions designed to help the implementation of the culture. In 1995, when the rest of the staff are involved, there will be relatively few aspects still to be discussed, but it will be clear that their active involvement in these remaining elements is essential if the culture is to take root in the firm. There are examples throughout this book of organisations that have carefully tailored their messages to the different layers of management and staff.

Checklist

In this chapter, Plot Your Route, we have touched on three main elements of effective communication:

1. *Research*. It is essential to establish how effectively the organisation is communicating at present, and the attitudes of the people concerned to the messages which are reaching them.

   Research can also be a powerful tool in enlisting the support of senior members of the management team.

   In planning research, be clear about your objectives and choose the most suitable form of quantitative or qualitative methods.

2. *Leadership*. Ensure that the most senior executives allocate enough time to communicating the message, and that their enthusiasm is captured and relayed to the entire audience.

   The leaders should also 'walk the talk' by demonstrating that they personally are applying the new policies.

3. *Tailor the message*. Decide in advance which elements of the message are most relevant to the different levels of the organisation and invite them to debate and implement those aspects to which they can best contribute.

4

Shoot the Pianist – Rover, United Distillers

'Our problem has been to create effective communications in a company that combines centuries-old tradition, with the latest in production technology working in every world time zone and in dozens of different cultural environments.' This was the challenge perceived by Phil Radcliff, HRD manager for United Distillers, one of the case study companies in this chapter.

United Distillers (UD) is a company that has grown rapidly over the last decade through acquisition and strategic partnerships. The real issue for UD has been to create a single set of shared values, language and ways of working from a pot-pourri of companies with very different corporate and cultural backgrounds.

Our other case here focuses on Rover, a company who underwent a merger and unification process many years ago. In the case of Rover, the culture that had crystallised by the mid-1980s was strongly product oriented with all communications and decision making achieved through a strictly hierarchical organisation with a high degree of centralisation. Fred Coultas, now Managing Director of the Motor Heritage Motor Centre, who has played a number of key roles in Rover says, 'In 1986, Rover's reputation as a maker of quality cars was almost a joke. We needed to initiate a process of change which would turn the company upside down to focus on people, both customers and workforce, and to ensure that all processes were simple and business oriented. We needed to develop a culture that provided a central framework but which encouraged local adaptation.'

Both companies faced considerable challenges. Too often, when there's something new and controversial to communicate, the old routines come into play, the usual old techniques are used, and nothing really gets through. Companies tend to slip into the same old routine of communications which is repeated year after year without any real analysis of whether they are achieving the desired effect. The Chairman's annual address, the in-house newspaper, the quarterly video update and many other communications devices become established as part of the fabric. When a new, important message is generated it is often forced out through these channels and fails. The old tunes are not necessarily the best. New messages often require new melodies and accelerated rhythms.

Both United Distillers and Rover needed to create a considerable cultural change within their own organisations in order to accommodate changes both within their organisational structures and the market-places they serve. Both companies recognised that large-scale cultural change is a long-term exercise and took considerable care to design comprehensive programmes to meet these challenges.

The two companies embarked on ambitious and innovative schemes which sought to gain the full involvement of all staff. They both followed almost textbook approaches, coupled with their own flair. However, there is at least one clear difference between the strategies of the two which is worth identifying at the outset.

In the previous chapter we started to look at the role of the top executives in initiating, designing, presenting and maintaining large-scale communications exercises. The contributions of Sir Anthony Cleaver at AEA Technology and Peter Davis at PW MCS were essential for the success of the programmes. Tony Greener and Crispin Davis at UD, and Graham Day and John Towers at Rover were also strong top teams, but they approached the problems of culture change in different ways as will be seen in the case studies.

Research has shown us that good communications can only be accomplished by paying careful attention to the answers to eight seemingly obvious but usually neglected questions:

1. Who is the audience?
2. Exactly what should the message be?

3. Who should do the communicating?
4. Where will the message be received?
5. What media will be most effective?
6. How can the message be reinforced?
7. What action is expected?
8. How long should the message be?

At the end of this chapter we will look at how well UD and Rover addressed these questions and with what observable results.

Rover – Moving into the fast lane

History

The Rover story is an extraordinary tale of a complete turnaround in the fortunes of a key contributor to the manufacturing sector of Great Britain. The company's move from near collapse to a prime position in the UK market has been brought about by careful attention to a well-designed communications programme that has reached not only all sections of the company but also many of the group's suppliers.

The Rover group is the present-day manifestation of a large part of motor manufacturing history in the British Isles. The marques owned by the group include many of the best-known and loved vehicles in motoring history from the early Austins, Morrises, Wolseys, Rileys and MGBs through the Minis, Maxis and Montegos and on to the 400s, 600s, 800s and Sterlings of today. In the 1960s and 1970s it had been the focus of major industrial unrest. The various amalgamations and reorganisations under Michael Edwards and others only seemed to delay the apparent inevitable slip into industrial decline.

By the mid-1980s the company's reputation had reached an all-time low. The range of vehicles was regarded as poorly designed and badly produced. The workforce of more than 52,000 was demoralised and producing fewer than half a million vehicles per year. The company was loss-making and the balance sheet was weak. Since 1986 this situation has been reversed: the workforce has been reduced to 33,000, the number of vehicles produced has exceeded half a million per year even during a recession market and the company's reputation for quality and performance is strong with customers and the City. Indeed the company has become so strong that in 1993 it was taken over by one of the world's prestige car manufacturers, BMW.

Many commentators have sought to explain this revival in Rover by pointing to the acquisition of new manufacturing technology and the importation of 'Japanese know-how' through joint ventures with Honda. However, this is a simplistic view of the changes that have taken place within the Rover group. Technology alone can make very little difference to a large manufacturing organisation. It is the skills, attitudes and commitment of the workforce using the technology that guarantees results. Rover has invested at least as much in communication and training as it has in installing automation.

Plotting the route

When Graham Day joined Rover in 1986 he brought with him a commitment to quality and a commitment to communication. He recognised that traditional Western manufacturing businesses shared a number of negative criteria:

- The structure of such companies tended to be full of both lateral and vertical barriers, blocking the flow of information and expertise from one level or one section to another. In some businesses there were as many as 14 levels of vertical barrier. It was not surprising that key messages sometimes lost their impact when required to cascade down that far or that the voices of the workforce were often muffled from senior management by the layers of sponge above them.

- All business activities in the company were profit driven
  rather than product focused. Issues of accountancy masked
  the essential considerations of market demand, product
  design and quality.
- Such companies tended to have massive business processes
  which had grown up over time and which actively interfered
  with effective communications and efficient management of
  the business.

Graham Day's intention was to turn the business on its head by
making people a priority, by clear product targeting and by
ensuring that all processes were simple and directly business
related. The central thrust of the new scheme can be summarised
as a classic total quality management (TQM) programme. He
recognised that there is a very high level of inertia which can
act against such a substantial re-engineering of a corporate
culture which has developed across decades. He understood
that he was embarking on a project in which the planned
changes were expected to take five or six years to complete.

He perceived a number of key changes that needed to be
made in the culture and processes of the organisation. The
culture and processes needed to reflect:

Culture	Processes
Dedication to truth	Added value
Leadership, motivation and enthusiasm from the top	Minimum interfaces
Shared values	Zero duplication
Business orientation	All factholders involved as a norm
Common objectives	Longer horizons for all
Effective communication	Integrated systems
Commitment to quality	Parallel/team working
A learning environment	Broader resources
Objectivity	Shorter cycles

The first task was to gain unequivocal support from the Rover board. Some of the incumbents were extremely sceptical of the changes that were being proposed. They felt comfortable with the traditional view that managers make all the decisions and that the workforce on the line is there to do as it is told. They were fearful of a change towards a position where all workers were encouraged and empowered to contribute to the decision-making process and where the management role become more of a coach and adviser than an authoritarian. However, Graham Day brought into the organisation a number of new directors who shared his views on organisational structure and communications. Among these were John Towers, now Chief Executive of Rover Group, who joined from Massey Ferguson and George Simpson, Managing Director, who came in from Leyland DAF.

Graham Day also strongly held the view that leadership should not be the sole province of the Chief Executive but should be through ideas and should be the province of everybody in the company. The new initiative was to be called 'Success Through People'. He and the executive team believed that 'People make differences and our people are different.' He had seen too many grand schemes grind to a halt when the single charismatic leader moved on or lost interest. In the case of Rover this was almost prescient since Day himself moved on to the Chairman's role at British Aerospace in 1990 with Rover's culture change programme still in its infancy.

The three main planks of initiating the TQM initiative were:

- empowerment
- training
- teamwork.

Choosing communicators

Of course, the senior managers were brought into the process at an early stage. Three hundred top executives were gathered in a senior management 'scrum' where many of the ideas were thrashed out. These sessions were externally facilitated by PA Associates who helped to ensure that the managers concentrated on developing a clear business agenda which could be implemented. The first outcome from these meetings was a recognition that everybody in the company needed a first immersion in the new culture as quickly as possible.

Six senior managers were seconded to the TQM team for six months to demonstrate commitment from the board. PA developed a series of workshops and materials to explain the changes. A total of 40,000 people experienced three days of intensive training in TQM.

A simple course alone cannot have the effect of breaking down long-term resistance and changing attitudes overnight. The essential factor was to explain the goals of the programmes to people so they could measure the company's commitment and progress towards it. One of the greatest difficulties for a scheme of this kind, particularly in large-scale organisations, is that there are generally three different types of reaction.

1. There are the 'innovators' who immediately see the benefits of the change and are committed overnight. They become the catalysts for moving the process forward.
2. There are the 'Luddites' who do not want to shift from the comfort of the world they know and are vociferous and seemingly committed enemies of change. This group does not present real problems. They identify themselves as challenges to be won over.
3. The third group are the most dangerous. These are the 'time servers' who will go along with anything that 'the management' say, for a quiet life. They lack real commitment and can provide the greatest resistance to change since they do not become involved.

Empowerment was the first main step for the entire workforce at Rover. One way of doing this was to change people's image of their roles by breaking down as many barriers in the company as possible. Some of the steps that were taken may seem trite but they were none the less effective. For example:

- All meaningless privileges, such as management restaurants and reserved parking, were dumped unless everybody could see that they had clear business or efficiency benefits. Some early attempts to dump them all actually decreased efficiency!
- The term 'employee' was dumped and everybody was viewed as an 'associate' of the company, with a stake in its future.
- Everybody, including the Chief Executive and senior managers, was asked to wear the same Rover uniform, with no badges of rank, when on site. Managers were encouraged to 'walk the talk', taking an interest in people on the line and their home lives and interests, as well as the specific functions they fulfil on the line.
- The company tried to become involved in issues outside day-to-day operations which related to the interests of associates. For example, near the plant at Swindon, Rover became involved with the local football club, seeking to bring people's home values and loyalties into the workplace.
- People were actively encouraged to put forward ideas for new systems, restructuring operations or improving design, safety or productivity. In Honda the average associate contributed eight ideas a year to the company. In Rover in 1990, on average each employee was still only contributing 0.6.
- Total honesty by management was promoted as a concept. This was not meant to imply that the management thought that all associates would always agree with what was being planned but there should be no nagging doubts or uncertainties which demotivate the workforce. In addition, associates may be able to make positive helpful suggestions.

All of this has perhaps been best illustrated by the commitment to 'employment for life'. In 1990, as part of the 'Rover

Tomorrow' exercise, John Towers observed, 'There is nothing that makes people more willing to contribute to company development than security.' The positive benefits brought by job security and an expectation of employment for life to the levels of commitment, contribution and feeling of ownership of the enterprise that people experienced were immediately apparent. By 1992 the company was able to make good this promise by ending compulsory redundancy.

Training was the second major element of the plan. The traditional British view has been that training is something done to you, probably only once, and you then have to find your own way. Rover was committed to the establishment of a complete learning environment. This means a great deal more than merely providing associates with the specific skills they need to complete their allocated tasks. It means ensuring that everybody is committed to continual development. This is not just the development of work skills. It also means the development of knowledge and interest in other areas of their lives. It does not just mean improving themselves but recognising that they also have a role to play in developing their colleagues and the organisation as a whole.

The company set up 'The Rover Learning Business' under Fred Coultas to co-ordinate a complete training strategy which would involve everything from TQM issues, through specific skills training and on to encouraging the acquisition of skills that were not specifically job-related, such as languages, pastimes and sports. In addition to work-related training, every associate could claim grants through the REAL (Rover Employer-Assisted Learning) scheme for these outside activities and would often match the leisure time devoted by the associate with time off from normal work.

Initial reactions to these schemes were very mixed. The traditionalists could not understand why the company should act in this charitable way. However, by 1990 more than 3,000 associates had taken part in the REAL scheme and the increase in commitment to the company that they showed convinced many of the sceptics.

Teamwork is the third key element. The entire structure of the company was reformulated into cells which are organised around a cell leader and encouraged both to take high levels of responsibility for the ways in which they work and to design their own working processes to best suit local need. The philosophy is 'central framework – local adaptation'.

A wide variety of different teams are fostered within the organisation. Of particular importance have been the inter-disciplinary teams in product design, where major savings of time and improvements in performance have been noted.

Teams have taken great pride of ownership in projects under their control. An excellent example of this would be the installation of new body presses at Swindon. The team to be responsible for the new equipment visited Japan to discuss the operation of the equipment with the manufacturers and to take part in the commissioning process. The eventual result of this team ownership was the efficient installation of the equipment within three months rather than the nine months for previous typical installations.

Sometimes team pride can be slightly negative. Often, in the past, when a team came up with an entirely innovative and efficient approach they would keep it to themselves since it made their team look better than others. The challenge is to persuade individuals to balance their pride in their own team's performance with an overall pride in contribution to the enterprise. The 'copy plus' system, formally introduced in 1992, encourages teams to share their ideas with the rest of the organisation. Under the copy plus system, new ideas, products and processes are shared readily. However, if another team manages a further improvement they are required to recognise the source of the original idea and to instruct the original team in the improvement that has been added. This way, everybody benefits.

The types of changes that John Towers wishes to make, and believes the emphasis on empowerment, training and teams can achieve, can be set out as follows:

Today	Tomorrow	The Future
Management directs	People suggest	People push management for change
Customers concerned about	All Rover concerned about	Everybody works on quality at all times

Count the cost

For Rover, the best way of counting the cost is to measure their improvements against the bench-marks of other organisations. The Rover team spends a great deal of effort in bench-marking a variety of elements in the process such as:

- quality
- asset base
- inventory
- logistics
- productivity
- teamwork
- staff turnover
- attitudes
- training.

In addition, the company does not only benchmark within the motor sector by looking at Ford and Honda, but looks at other successful organisations such as Barclays, Savacentre and Motorola. Regular independent reviews are carried on within the company to evaluate progress.

Summary

This is a case study of a total communications process. The actual means applied in delivering the communications were as varied as the numbers of groups and teams that took part. The company certainly produced or commissioned core learning materials but it always expected these to be adopted and adapted at will by the target audiences. The main conclusion about this case is the clear design process of the original philosophy and a recognition of the time that it takes to implement such a major change process in a complex traditional organisation.

Has it worked? Well, the answer that Rover managers give you is 'Take a look at the balance sheet.' They are now a strong successful profitable company. However, the real success, of which the financial performance is only a reflection, is the attitude of the workforce. If you talk to them they will tell you that they used to avoid admitting that they worked for BMC, or Leyland or Austin. Today they are proud of their company and want to tell everybody about it.

Since 1986, have they achieved everything that they set out to accomplish? Of course not. In some areas they have achieved more and in some they have still to make real inroads. The 'not invented here' brigade still exist. The time servers are still there making less than committed contributions but their time is running out.

John Towers states it starkly, 'Nobody has legislated for Rover to be around in a few years time. Success is not mandatory. It has to be created by the whole team working together. We have to become a world–class team with a future.' It looks as though, with their commitment to total communications, they already are.

United Distillers – Blending the right spirit

History

In 1992 United Distillers was the most profitable alcoholic beverage company in the world. Its range of brands read like a roll–call of the world's best spirits, including blended whiskies such as Johnnie Walker, Bell's, Dewars and White Horse, American bourbons such as IW Harper, the top quality white spirits of Tanqueray and Gordons gins, famous brandies such as Asbach, right through to best–selling rums such as Pampero from Venezuela. Its marketing operations and joint ventures covered the world from Europe to the USA, from Africa to the Far East and incorporated the world-famous Hennessey.

However, the period from the formation of the group in 1986 had not exactly been calm and controlled. United Distillers, an operating division of the Guinness group, has come about through a series of take-overs, acquisitions and joint ventures starting with the merger of Distillers Company Ltd with a number of traditional distillers such as Arthur Bell, through partnerships with producers and distributors including a major strategic alliance with Louis Vuitton Moët Hennessey, and was then forced to survive the troubled times of the take-over by the Guinness Group.

The challenge

By 1991, United Distillers (UD) had not developed into a single, stable, coherent organisation but still existed as a loose agglomeration of different companies, each with its own history, systems, approaches, values and beliefs. The company had grown in size substantially, more than doubling its workforce. Profit performance had quadrupled. The company had become truly international and had developed its range of brands. However, the position was fragile. Tony Greener, the Chief Executive, and the Executive Committee had a vision of the way in which UD should develop to secure success as the major player in the world spirits market. They recognised that the development of shared values and approaches as well as improved management systems would be essential to achieve this end. It was immediately obvious that a number of key issues needed to be addressed quickly. Most of the UK-based companies that had been acquired or merged to make up UD had three clear characteristics.

Firstly, they tended to possess strong, traditional, paternalistic management cultures. The original companies had been strong individual brand operations. Strangely, although there were usually well-laid down management procedures, systems and authority, they often lacked clearly defined, effective management processes. Bringing them together resulted in a high degree of centralisation which resulted in a lack of consultation and poor teamwork. The climate within these companies often tended to be insecure, suspicious and uncertain. All control of these businesses came from the centre and since information was regarded as a source of power, it was held with high levels of secrecy. Relationships between managers and subordinates were non-consultative. Teamwork was almost non-existent. There was a strong task focus with limited performance management and little individual feedback. Many individuals were uncertain about the identity of the company and could not understand their position within the overall process.

Secondly, the original companies had been brand oriented. The great traditions of some of the UD brands were clearly important and valuable assets. However, brand loyalty could act against effective marketing of the full range of the company's products. There was a move towards portfolio management of the business. Now, the key task was clearly to build on the strengths of the brands within this more comprehensive marketing strategy. The need was to promote portfolio marketing on a global basis.

Thirdly, whether they were based in Scotland, England, Germany, France, Venezuela, the USA, Australia or elsewhere in the world their vision was often limited by national boundaries. UD was now a global marketing organisation operating through four regions with a need to understand the requirements of each market separately and an ability to communicate effectively between different cultures, working in different time zones and in different languages.

Plotting the route

The UD Executive recognised that changing the culture of a
single company cannot be achieved overnight. A new culture
cannot be bought off a shelf. Changing the cultures of dozens
of companies to weld them into a coherent whole is an even
more difficult task. New values cannot be imposed on people.
They need to understand how the values being proposed will
help them to achieve the business targets that they are being
set. Old values are not dislodged by decree but rather through
observation and positive experience. The most important role
model is always that of the company's leaders, the members of
the executive management group and the board. Unless they
are seen to be providing clear leadership by example, culture
change is doomed to failure.

The Executive Committee understood the need to achieve
consensus with the top management group in the company.
They also realised the difficulties of attempting to achieve this
through internal resources alone. Too often, internal facilitators
and communicators are thought to be following their own
agendas and are not entirely trusted. UD recognised that it
needed to form partnerships with external consultants. Greg
Spiro Associates (GSA), a management consultancy with a
proven track record of working with the top management of
blue-chip companies in defining and refining strategic plans,
was appointed to develop effective methodologies managing
change. Greg Spiro worked intensively with the UD Executive
to develop a clear picture of the company's strategic requirements. While care was taken to look forward towards the new
vision of the company, great care was taken in all these
discussions to balance the different backgrounds of the consti-
tuent companies and to be sensitive to the market and cultural
imperatives which exist in different countries and territories.

This required a framework and methodology. The discussions were always lively, often exposing strong differences of
view which needed to be resolved. Sometimes significant
obstacles seemed to be identified such as the dichotomy

between a traditional manufacturing-oriented culture and a modern marketing-directed environment. However, the commitment of the team to developing a clear lead for the company as a whole eventually led to a clearly defined culture statement. This culture statement was called 'the UD Way'. This took the form of:

- a succinct business *mission* which crystallised all the main elements that the company expected to achieve on behalf of the stakeholders
- eight clear *core values* which they felt needed to be understood and owned by everybody. These were felt to be the keys to business success and to a feeling of pride which everyone should have in the company, ensuring that they all work together as a team with a set of unifying goals. The core values headings are: inheritance, standards, people, common purpose, internationalism, communities, social responsibility and environment.

  It can be seen without difficulty that some of them: inheritance, people, common purpose, standards and internationalism, would be easy to assimilate directly into the business because they make clear contributions to the traditional views of business success. However, the other values of social responsibility, environment and community are equally important for the achievement of the business mission. It is not merely that they are 'nice' to do; the directors of UD believed that companies that do not pay attention to the key social issues around them which affect their markets may find themselves with declining overall performance in the long term. UD is a business which looks towards a long future and those working in it at any particular time are viewed as the stewards of the culture. (It should be noted that the core values stated above are only summary headings. The actual value statements were far more extensive and detailed.)
- 10 *operating principles*. A large international company needs a framework of structures, processes and procedures so that

everybody can do their jobs effectively. Within such a framework, the company believes that adopting a set of fundamental principles to guide behaviour will lead to competitive advantage through outstanding performance and a great sense of pride and commitment among all employees. The adoption of these principles throughout the organisation depends not only on leadership by management, but also on their application by everyone in the business. The UD Operating Principles are: performance, recognition, excellence, delegation, openness, teamwork, communication, innovation, balance and sensitivity. One appears in the UD Way in the form illustrated:

Operating Principles—
Communications

7 *The highest standards of communication as a key to organisational effectiveness.*

Having defined the mission, core values and operating principles, it was felt to be important for all senior members of the management team to review how well they demonstrated, reflected and maintained their belief in them. This was achieved through a series of coaching sessions between Greg Spiro and the directors based on peer review, and by confidential upward assessment of directors by their subordinates against the operating principles. This work led to the management of behaviour at the top of the business and a series of processes which could be adopted by all managers.

It was recognised early in the process that the existing communications channels within the organisation were not sufficient on their own to carry the message of the UD Way and to ensure that it would gain credibility. Greg Spiro, Mike Pemberton (the Personnel Director) and Phil Radcliff (the Human Resources Development Manager), felt that it was important that the next step be to consult senior managers throughout the organisation on the UD Way, to gain their advice and to enlist their assistance in designing and delivering the message in an innovative and interesting manner.

During 1991 and early 1992, team workshops were held around the world with all managers. At these workshops, managers were introduced to the mission, core values and operating principles and were asked to comment on the relevance of these to their sectors of the company and how they felt that the introduction of the UD Way would either benefit or hinder the achievement of their business targets and team performance.

Initially, there was clearly a high degree of scepticism about the introduction of such a far-reaching scheme apparently from on high. One of the greatest complaints from managers was that, although the company now professed internationalism, the majority of decision making, it seemed, was still made back in the UK without full appreciation of the difficulties of implementation in widespread international markets. The overall concern was that the UD Way would be just another fine-sounding public relations initiative from the centre of the company that would have little relevance to achieving the stated business goals.

However, during the seminars, which were predominantly run by Greg Spiro and Phil Radcliff with a few additional trained facilitators, managers were encouraged to look at the core values and operating principles one by one and to discuss how each fitted in with their local business needs. A number of tools were devised by Radcliff and Spiro to aid the workshops. The first was a 'Managers' Guide' to the UD Way, which clearly defined each value and principle and then illustrated the latter by suggesting behaviours that would be 'in character' and those that would be 'out of character' if the UD Way had been implemented fully. The following table illustrates this point.

From the 'Managers' Guide' to the UD Way

Action Guidelines – Principle Seven

'The highest standards of communication as a key to organisational effectiveness'

Clarification

Effective communication is the central factor in good decision-making and the implementation of decisions. Openness, feed-back, recognition, delegation and teamwork are some of the main characteristics of good communications. The promotion of trust, building motivation and establishing confidence all rely on effect-ive communications.

Everybody in UD therefore needs to develop their communication and interpersonal skills. Where possible communication should always be two-way to allow for feedback which will improve the analysis of effectiveness, the exchange of information and to provide an opportunity for learning new techniques and improv-ing future communications.

Communications need to be adapted to match the needs, abilities and expectations of the parties concerned. For this reason, communications should be adapted to the style of local cultures and good practice should be pursued in the many foreign languages used by UD in addition to English.

*Behaviours are **in** character when we:*

- clearly identify the audiences for our communications and take into account their needs
- plan our communications to take account of our colleagues' schedules, and respond to communications in time to allow action to be taken in a way that allows for the time differences that exist when operating worldwide.
- seek to develop a working competence in the languages of the key staff and markets with whom we communicate
- demonstrate and seek to improve our range and standards of communication skills in both one-to-one and group situations
- are able to communicate a well-argued business case in writing
- are able to articulate and frame cases or discuss issues clearly and succinctly.

*Behaviours are **out of** character when we:*

- fail to keep our staff informed of key decisions or strategic developments within the company

- insist on using a single method of communication because it suits us, rather than paying attention to the recipient of the communication
- communicate only in English with no regard to either the language or the cultural characteristics of the audience
- are discourteous to members of staff, to colleagues in joint venture companies or to clients
- demonstrate poor communication skills
- are unwilling or unable to present clear sets of recommendations in writing.

*Attitudes are **in** character when we:*

- believe that clear communications are essential to the effective management of the business
- understand the need for two-way communication
- want to learn the languages and cultural approaches of the staff and customers with whom we need to communicate.

*Attitudes are **out of** character when we:*

- think that everybody in the company should communicate in the manager's own language, and take no account of the global nature of the company
- believe that it is the responsibility of others to interpret communications, rather than our responsibility to take account of others' needs
- believe that memos are always the right way to communicate information.

*Outcomes are **in** character when:*

- everybody feels they have all the information they need
- communications arrive in the best form for the recipient to understand, in terms of language, medium and level of expression
- people are confident that they are well-informed and that the company is being honest with them
- everybody understands that clear communication will enhance their effectiveness.

*Outcomes are **out of** character when:*

- communications arrive too late to be taken into account in decision making, although deadlines were clear
- people feel that information is being kept from them.

The second tool was a series of scenarios derived from actual incidents that had taken place within the company. Participants in the workshops were asked to identify out of character behaviour, to suggest what actions should have been taken to be in character and then to analyse the business benefits.

Although the result was not universal support for the programme, a considerable proportion of the managers who were won over were excited by the UD Way and were enthusiastic that they were being asked to contribute to its development and that they would eventually be involved in tailoring the approach to their own areas provided that the central message was maintained.

Each workshop contributed more ideas and potential adaptation to the UD Way as a whole and the team at the centre were continually revising documentation and discussing new approaches. One of the biggest problems of entering into such an extensive consultation process was the amount of time that it required. The workshops themselves generated a great deal of enthusiasm which was then often frustrated by the need to postpone the next step until full agreement had been achieved world-wide.

Eventually, after almost a year of workshops and consultation it was decided by the Executive Committee that, although it was hoped and expected that the UD Way would continue to develop, the time had come to cascade the principles of the UD Way to all areas of the business before enthusiasm and support disappeared.

This would also coincide with two other changes. A design company, The Michael Peters Group, had been asked to develop a new corporate identity which had just been agreed upon and it would clearly be helpful if this design formed an integral part of the UD Way to be rolled out through normal management channels. Secondly, Tony Greener had become Chairman and Chief Executive of the Guinness Group and had been succeeded as chief executive on the UD Executive Committee by Crispin Davis, a marketing-oriented executive, with a background in Procter and Gamble. Clearly, the support of the new Chief Executive would be essential for progress of the UD Way and conversely, his position within an international exercise of this kind could help to cement his position.

UD called in Workhouse to develop a communications plan with Greg Spiro and Phil Radcliff. The consultant, the HRD manager and the communications company formed a strong partnership, with each providing a vital element to the process.

It was decided that the communications process could be achieved most readily by devising a tool-kit of media elements and activities which managers in different companies and different parts of the world could use to develop approaches which were relevant to their business needs. The overall strategy would be to start with those elements of the UD Way, core values or operating principles, having the highest priority in each region.

One of the earliest tasks was to decide on the extent of the audience to be addressed by this process. In common with many other companies today, the operating boundaries of UD are not absolutely clear. The traditional, original companies are wholly owned by UD. In addition, some of the joint venture partnerships had clearly become essential parts of the company. It could be questioned whether the joint venture with Louis Vuitton Moët Hennessy should make their employees part of the group who should understand the UD Way. Conversely, how should the UD Way be communicated to the parent group Guinness?

Although benefits could be seen from extending a basic understanding of the values and principles as far as possible, it was decided at this stage to limit the roll-out process to wholly owned subsidiaries of the company, with briefings at appropriate levels to the joint venture partners.

The team from UD, GSA and Workhouse, worked hard both to design the materials that would help promote the UD Way and to suggest a process which would ensure consistency of message while giving maximum flexibility of approach. Feedback suggested that there were clearly a number of key factors which needed to guide this work:

- The message should come from all parts of the company; from all the different operational sectors such as adminis- tration, production, marketing and finance as well as from all the different territories and cultures.
- The message needed explaining in simple credible terminology which would not appear to be simply a piece of 'head office propaganda'. It would be important for UD staff to express the culture in their own words.
- The message needed to be structured in such a way that it could be tailored to meet the needs and priorities of different markets.

An intensive research period was needed by the Workhouse team. During this period it was essential to have a single major link point within the company to facilitate the arrangement of meetings, visits and the explanation of the specific aspects of UD operations. However, two other issues arose during this research period. Firstly, the strong regional structure meant that the individual regions had strong identities and a clear sense of their own business priorities. These had to be carefully integrated into the mission and vision of the UD Way to establish appropriate levels of support to the global exercise. This required extensive efforts from Crispin Davis, the Chief Executive, and Mike Pemberton, the Personnel Director, in particular. Secondly, it was important that the new Chief Executive would readily exemplify the operating principles of the UD Way as well as support the communication pro- gramme.

Following the research period, the team designed the com- plete communication programme. The tool-kit comprised four text elements plus OHPs, four different types of video and an audio tape.

The first major element was the 'Facilitators' Guide' pack. This pack was designed to help the managers who were being designated as responsible for the UD Way cascade process in their areas. The pack comprised a text folder, a copy of 'The Managers' Guide' and an audio tape. The folder contained advice and exercises to determine the best way of designing and running sessions which would have the most relevance to individual facilitator managers' regions or departments. The whole thrust of the guide was to be non-prescriptive but to provide the maximum support to managers, many of whom would be relatively inexperienced at running this type of session. The 'Managers' Guide' was the latest version of the detailed specification of the UD Way with clear definitions of the mission, core values and operating principles. This update was very important because, although many of the facilitators would have taken part in earlier workshops, there could have been a gap of more than a year since they had first been involved. Definitions and ideas had developed in the interim. For each principle, there was not only a definition but also a clarification, with examples of in character and out of character behaviours, attitudes and outcomes. The audio tape took the form of an edited discussion between Phil Radcliff and Greg Spiro reviewing some of their experiences in running workshops and giving helpful hints and advice.

Although the guide was not prescriptive, it was suggested that, although details might vary significantly between different locations, most cascade programmes should follow a similar course. Some parts of the company decided to run a series of short workshops dealing with the elements one at a time. Other areas decided to run extended one- or two-day sessions. However, the process almost always started with a clear introduction. At the start of this, the facilitator would probably show the video element entitled 'The Rationale'. This was an explanation, by the Chief Executive, and other UD staff at all levels and from all areas, about the nature of the UD Way, why they believed it was so important and discussing some of the concerns they felt about particular elements of the programme. This latter point is important since research had shown that an explicit identification of these concerns enhanced the credibility of the project as a whole.

Following 'The Rationale', the facilitator used OHPs provided in the pack to lead a discussion about why a global culture is important for a company like UD. It was suggested that everybody within the company was a 'cultural steward', responsible for maintaining the best and most progressive elements of the company's values. Where relevant, another video element was often used at this point. This was a series of short trigger videos featuring the domain leaders talking about the importance of the UD Way to their geographical or operational responsibilities. Only those triggers directly relevant to the group would normally be shown, though some groups used them all to understand the potential interaction between the needs of different areas. Discussions about values and principles were enhanced by reference to a text, which contained quotations collected from throughout the company illustrating the different elements of the UD Way, outlining the benefits of operating within the principles, and exploring some of the concerns about potential conflict between business targets and some aspects of the programme; these quotations are shown in the table on page 85.

Facilitators were then recommended to use a number of tools provided for determining which core values and operating principles were seen as most important to the group. At the end of this session, participants were issued with an 'Aide-mémoire' card summarising core values and operating principles.

One of the outcomes of the exercises recommended in the 'Facilitator's Guide' was the completion of a 'gap analysis'. This identified the differences between the ways in which the group felt that it should be working to conform to its needs within the UD Way and its current status. The actions needed to close the gap were specified and target dates were set. Feedback loops were set up so that facilitators could send this information back to the HRD unit at UD headquarters and a world picture could be built up. Groups were also encouraged

Nowadays we are all competing for the very best people and so those companies that show themselves to be most at sympathy with their communities are going to be able to draw the best people from those communities.

Barry Fitzgibbon

As well as the direct jobs a lot of the tradesmen work at the distillery and there's a big spin off on tourism too – we offer a facility to the community so that they can come in and use that space for charitable work etc.

Brian Bissett

Pampero has always been very close not only to our consumers but also to the general public in Venezuela and we have been participating in representative expressions of the Venezuelan way of life.

Juan Puig

One has to demonstrate a long-term commitment that doesn't portray a short-term profit taking exercise to the detriment of the employees and the country that you are working in.

Brian Castleton-Knight

Our long-term interest should be based on support from the society. Without having support from the society it can't be successful.

Shick Kim

to submit best ideas and practice for developing values and principles. The company wanted to become a learning organisation, sharing information throughout the whole group about the development of its culture.

Later sessions usually concentrated on the individual values or principles identified as being of highest priority. These sessions would normally take the form of viewing a video trigger. A set of individual triggers were produced for each value and another set for each operating principle. A typical trigger would take the form of one or more UD employees telling a story in their own words which illustrated the issue under review. The trigger would end with a statement or set of questions designed to stimulate discussion. Following dis-

cussion of the trigger issues, participants were given a text
scenario from the facilitator's pack, which described an actual
issue which had arisen in the company:

The increased pressure brought about by successful sales and
marketing compaigns has created space problems in a major
office location. There are now just too many people to fit into the
old structure of individual offices. In addition, there are serious
parking difficulties due to the allocation of spaces to senior
managers. Spaces which are often vacant.

The manager of the office has worked hard with representatives
of all the areas which are likely to be affected by change and, after
considerable discussions, it has been decided that the unit will
move to an open-plan system for everybody. In addition, because
of this, it has been decided that the building will become a no-
smoking area.

The changes have been well communicated to everybody and,
while many people are not really happy, they understand why it
has to be done.

Within a few weeks of implementation of the new system a new
senior manager is appointed to the unit. Without reference to any
of the team who planned the changes, he insists on the rebuilding
of offices for himself and his senior assistants which are even
larger than his predecessor had originally occupied. In addition,
he reserves six of the twelve available car parking spaces for
senior managers. The first that most staff know of this is when
they return to the office after a holiday weekend.

Names and locations were changed to protect the guilty!
Participants were asked to work out how the staff involved in
the scenario should have acted in order to best exemplify the
UD Way, to consider any pressures they might have experienced to behave otherwise and how these pressures might be
avoided. These scenarios usually acted as a useful entry point
for participants to raise issues which had occurred in their own
operating experience and to discuss how they should have
acted to stay 'in character' with the UD Way. Sessions of this
kind could be held on as many or as few values and principles
as were identified by the gap analysis as essential. Facilitators

were encouraged to feed back as much information as possible to Phil Radcliff, who would ensure that best practice would be publicised and disseminated.

Conclusion

The programme was launched in mid-1993. The expectation was that all 15,000 UD employees throughout the world would take part in sessions of this kind within a year from launch. The videos and text elements were translated into a variety of languages, including French, German, Spanish and Japanese. Materials were distributed to all operating units and companies. It can be seen that this programme involved excellent planning, considerable care in development, and a high level of investment, in both developing materials and briefing managers. Some countries took on the UD Way with enthusiasm and believe that they have benefited from working through the programme.

It is difficult to co-ordinate a global exercise and it rapidly devolves to local units to progress as they feel appropriate. The role of top management is critical, not just in supporting the communication programme but also in exemplifying the culture in their own style and behaviour.

With regard to the materials assembled, much of it is in extensive use in the business via programmes of coaching, colleague feedback and performance review. The video materials can be updated easily and the communication process can continue. The development of a corporate culture is a continuing process which needs to be nurtured for as long as the company is in existence.

Was the pianist shot?

At the beginning of this chapter we looked at the eight questions that need to be answered for the design of effective communications programmes (see page 61). To a large extent, both Rover and UD exerted considerable efforts to answer these questions in great detail.

They defined their audiences very carefully, considering from the outset the extent to which the message should be communicated to the extended enterprise. They recognised that while the core audience within the companies themselves were pre-eminently important, it was also vital that joint venture partners and suppliers should also understand the developments that were taking place.

Both organisations crafted the messages with care. The message was not only defined at the top levels but was tested with groups of key managers in workshops and 'scrums' before the final definition took place. The communications teams tried to ensure that the messages would not only be precisely defined but would also be expressed in terms that would be acceptable within the cultures to which they were to be delivered, and also that the messages would be credible and consistent with the demands of the business.

If properly trained, individual line managers can communicate most effectively at a local level by making sure that the central message is adapted to local conditions. In both companies a strong central framework was defined and high levels of local adaptation were encouraged.

In both companies, it was expected that the message would be delivered in a variety of different locations. The essence of this type of communication programme is that it eventually becomes a part of the fabric of normal business life. Both UD and Rover ran presentations, workshops and seminars for staff in formal locations. However, they also tried to ensure that the message would be constantly present on the line or in the offices. The cultural differences between the different world locations of UD are more obvious than those at Rover. However, within both organisations care had to be taken to arrange the presentations to suit local norms.

Neither of these organisations, nor their consultants, approached these exercises with any preconceived ideas about media. For some exercises in Rover the issue was not so much media as management training in communications. In both cases text proved to be a highly effective medium for carrying detailed information and acting as reference work. Video provided the opportunity for exciting the audiences and illustrating key operations. The key factor in selecting each medium was that it could be used effectively in the intended location and that it was an effective vehicle for carrying the type of message or stimulating the action required at the relevant part of the process.

In Rover, it was intended that the message be reinforced by the continuing commitment of the company to its staff, the improvements in product quality this would create and the response this would generate in customers. This commitment to staff would eventually lead to a growing sense of job security which is a highly motivating factor. It has worked. At the present stage of the roll-out at UD, it is difficult to identify whether reinforcement mechanisms are being brought into play effectively. It was intended that this should be carried out through regular employee communications systems by highlighting good practice and recognising and rewarding good practitioners.

Both organisations were clear about the action expected. They wanted nothing more nor less than a complete change of culture to match the changing needs of the markets within which they were working. However, at each stage, they both tried to define the steps along the way and the indicators that would be used to judge whether they had been achieved. This can be seen particularly in the 'gap analysis' exercises introduced by UD and in the constant, on-line, reviews of progress carried out by Rover. For both organisations the required actions needed to be defined on a local basis within the overall aim of culture change.

The final question was – 'How long should the message be?' Although individual elements need to be structured carefully, the simple answer for these two communications exercises as a whole is – 'For ever'. It is impossible to place limits on pro-

grammes which are designed to stimulate continued development. It should be a 'never-ending story'; if it reaches a
conclusion, it has probably failed.

Checklist

In this chapter, Shoot the Pianist, we have touched on four
main issues for successful implementation of large-scale communications:

1. *Design*. It is important to make sure that the communications message is clearly defined, its impact on the business
   identified and its delivery determined well before starting
   the process itself. Whenever possible there should be wide
   consultation with all sectors of the intended audience to
   ensure that the eventual programme will be sufficiently
   flexible to meet all needs.
2. *Co-ordination*. The most common factor in failed communications is the failure to recognise the resource requirements
   for co-ordinating the delivery and evaluation of communications. The best designed programmes will fail if there is
   not a strong central point to maintain momentum. This will
   often require the recruitment or secondment of one or more
   individuals full time.
3. *Role models*. Senior staff within an organisation are taken
   as the key role models. It is no use their mouthing support
   for a message or culture change if their behaviour is at
   variance. This places a strong responsibility on executives.
   Avoid the cult of personality. It is also important that the
   responsibility for role modelling is spread as widely as
   possible so that a communications process does not live or
   die by the behaviour or future of one individual alone.
4. *Patience*. Culture change, attitude change or process change
   nearly always take longer than expected. Changing long-
   term practices and traditions is rather like trying to stop or
   steer a supertanker. New corporate cultures cannot be

bought off the shelf. They take long-term investment in management and communications skills to establish them. Plan well at the outset, publish the plans and continue with them. Don't create uncertainties of direction by constant revision or by trying new options because the process is taking longer than expected.

■ Enrol Your Owners – BP, Courtaulds European Fibres, Meridian Broadcasting

At the heart of any communications programme lie the men and women who will present the message to staff at every level in the organisation, who will explain its content, field questions and lead discussions. In the best-run communications programmes, they will also plot the route forward, helping people formulate their own action plans for implementing the strategy or change programme and setting a timetable for monitoring and feeding back the results of those personal plans. The English language has still to find an elegant word to describe the role; 'facilitator' is commonly used as a name for the person who leads the discussion group; 'empowerment' describes the philosophy of involving managers in the process. The concept of 'enrolling your owners' addresses the need to involve facilitators, be they specialists or line managers, in both the message and its implementation.

This makes 'facilitation' an ugly word but a challenging task. Very few supervisors or middle managers have been trained in these skills; if we are honest, nor are many senior executives . . . We have witnessed a bank manager destroy the impact of a carefully prepared corporate communication by lifelessly reading out to the staff of his branch the words of a pre-prepared text, chin firmly glued to his collar bone, never a glance at his audience; he then shuffled his papers and rushed out of the room for fear that anyone might want to ask questions which could prove difficult to answer. We have heard managers ingratiate themselves with their audiences – but destroy the message – by throwing in off-the-cuff comments which imply that 'if you believe this, you'll believe anything'.

The result of such failures is a blockage in the process, a

clear breakdown in communications. Worse still, it can lead to resentment among those sections of the staff who have been deprived of their chance to participate in the process. Depressingly, more communications programmes fail because the facilitators are insufficiently skilled or motivated than for any other reason.

In this chapter we shall be relating three case studies, all successful in both enrolling their owners and in empowering their managers to pass the message from senior management to the most junior of staff, each of them using a different approach and process.

British Petroleum (BP) prepared the ground carefully for a major change in the organisational culture of the group; it empowered all its managers to communicate with their staff in all parts of the world and provided them with the support they needed; the culture change survived the departure of the Chairman and Chief Executive who had initiated the programme and helped BP weather the buffeting it received during the recession of the early 1990s.

Courtaulds started from the bottom up, introducing cell briefings at plant level through which routine management messages are regularly passed. When it came to a major event, the joint merger of its Fibres Division with that of Hoechst in Germany, the pathway was prepared for an important one-off communication. Courtaulds also illustrates the radically different cultures within which the German and Spanish arms of the merger have to communicate.

Meridian Broadcasting had just over a year in which to establish a brand-new television operation; it had no tradition of communication on which to draw and relied on a small team of experienced communicators to explain its philosophy to every person joining the company.

Each adopted a different approach, suited to the culture of the company and the circumstances of the communication. Each succeeded where nine out of ten companies appear to fail. There isn't a single recommended route, but there are lessons to be learned from all of them, as we shall see.

BP – Project 1990

When Robert Horton stepped into the joint posts of Chairman and Chief Executive of BP in March 1990, he had already prepared plans for sweeping changes in the organisation, most notably at head office. He had decided to reduce radically the 'brigadier belt', the managers whose function appeared to him to comprise receiving, acknowledging and passing on paperwork. He also wanted to eliminate the 'nanny knows best' philosophy which tied the hands of BP's operating companies.

Up to that point, the line management had little power to take action unless authorised from above; there was too much second guessing of business judgements by the head office in London.

'Project 1990', as it was dubbed, became a milestone in the history of Britain's change management. At the time, BP was perceived to be on an even keel, one of Britain's largest companies, secure in the knowledge that when its downstream businesses were doing poorly its upstream operations were likely to be doing well, and vice versa. Horton planned his shake-up at a time when there was no overwhelming external reason for doing so; he wanted to make BP more flexible and responsive to possible surprises in the 1990s. Indeed, it was not long before BP had to face two events which were to test the new philosophy to the limit.

The first was the 1992 recession, 'the most unfavourable external environment facing the oil industry since national-isation'. The second was Horton's abrupt departure from the company, an event unparalleled in BP's history. In theory, either of these crises should have thrown the change pro-gramme off course. In fact, Project 1990 appears to have survived both and, in 1994, BP emerged as the company which received the most favourable press in Britain, ousting Tescos and Marks and Spencer from the top spot in the Presswatch poll.

Bold strokes, long march

'Bold strokes, long march' is how Kate Owen describes the
philosophy which carried Project 1990 through the buffeting it
was to receive. She and Ian Howell were key players in the
project – Owen was a member of the Culture Change Team
responsible for implementing the change; Howell had been a
member of the Project 1990 Team with particular responsibility for communicating the change across BP.

The project management team had been formed in mid-1989
when Horton first knew he had been selected to take the top
post. As Chris Lorenz described this in the *Financial Times* it
had not been picked from the ranks of the powerful managing
directors of BP's main businesses whose roles were to
be rigorously examined and redefined. Instead, following
common practice in BP, a team of rising executives – five men
and two women aged between 35 and 40 – had been specially
selected to work under David Pascall, a Divisional Manager in
BP Finance. Horton set the Project 1990 team three goals:

- to refine the structure
- to simplify processes
- to establish a new culture and style.

The group set out to investigate best practice and the best
practitioners of corporate change. At the time they found very
little on this side of the Atlantic – a reflection of the speed with
which change management has since become an accepted part
of management. In the UK companies like Mars and Rank
Xerox had designed and communicated new corporate philosophies but not on this scale and not to this degree of change. In
the US, on the other hand, a number of large organisations –
like General Electric under Jack Welch – had radically
changed their organisation and culture, and academics like
Rosbeth Moss Kanter had written textbooks on change management. Pascall and his team went to America to meet Welch

and others; they also held discussions with pundits at the world's leading business schools.

In September 1989, the group conducted interviews with over 500 managers at various levels within BP around the world; this was followed by a wide-scale survey of the attitudes of BP's staff. One in six of the company's professional and management grades were invited to fill in questionnaires; more than 4,000 were returned representing a healthy 65 per cent response.

The results of both surveys demonstrated that the company was still regarded as secure, wealthy, commercially oriented and with good business growth prospects – no one had yet spotted the imminence of the devastating recession. However, the surveys also revealed weaknesses in career satisfaction and the management systems. The company was seen as over-complex with unclear lines of authority and cumbersome decision making. There was no clear group mission; inefficiency and short-termism were rampant. Internal communications were poor, bottom up and top down, across functions and across businesses. Crucially, the surveys showed that staff believed the company paid more or less the right degree of attention to its shareholders and customers and even to the communities in which it operated but that it ignored the interests of its own staff. There was insufficient attention paid to personal development; creativity and initiative were stifled by mistrust, criticism and fear of risk taking.

The Project 1990 team fed their conclusions back to Horton in November 1989. They reported their fear that BP was in danger of becoming 'the dinosaur of the 1990s'. The findings confirmed Horton's own views: BP suffered from confused messages, a lack of clear vision, excessive emphasis on asset trading, and lack of pride. He diagnosed that the group was in drastic need of clear vision, continuous innovation, open communication, empowered people, deep trust and team accountability.

'Horton declared that he wanted to create what he described as "the corporate equivalent of perestroika and glasnost" . . .

the result was to be a structure with the minimum of controls and the maximum delegation of responsibility, plus a supporting culture of openness, informal communication and verve.' These words are taken from a series of articles written by Chris Lorenz in *The Financial Times*; Lorenz had been afforded the remarkable privilege of being allowed to observe a senior management seminar, held in December 1989 at the Compleat Angler in Marlow, and attended by all but one of the company's top 28 executives.

The Compleat Angler

It was at this seminar that Project 1990 was unveiled to BP's top management. One hundred and sixty head office jobs would disappear out of 540 – small beer compared with the job losses which would be caused by the recession but startling at a time when there was no external pressure on the company. Tiers of management would be eliminated and many long-established committees would be disbanded.

More importantly, BP would launch a series of programmes right across the group aimed directly at changing attitudes and behaviour to fit the changed work relationships. Horton expected the change to take two or three years ('perhaps optimistically', observed Lorenz at the time).

'Significantly,' wrote Lorenz, 'for the nature of the blueprint – but also for the resistance which some of it had provoked before the meeting – the work for Project 1990 has been done not by the corporate barons themselves or their nominees. Instead it had been handled by Horton's own nominee . . . Signally silent through long phases of the discussion are some of the older managing directors. Some Managing Directors seemed clearly uncomfortable with the degree of change being proposed . . . despite Horton and the Project 1990 team having worked with them continuously behind the scenes during the months before Marlow . . . Their discomfort was caused not merely by the impact of changes on their own roles.

It was also because of the strong message that there must be a
radical streamlining of the company's structure and its management processes but also of its culture.'

By Lorenz' account, the Compleat Angler was an extraordinary event. Nearly 30 senior managers were invited to
debate a radically new corporate culture. They all appreciated
the need for change – the survey had provided a demonstration
of that – and many had been consulted on the details of the
proposals. The sheer size of the senior management team left
little opportunity at this stage for a real debate on the detail.
The very presence of an outside journalist, however favourable
his account might turn out to be, suggested a boldness and
determination to motor the changes through. In an organisation as large as BP it is hard to think of another way to
introduce change at this level; we have seen from other case
studies how important it is to secure the full support of senior
colleagues before a change programme is launched and, in an
ideal world, the seminar format is better suited either to the
formulation of a change strategy, with genuine input from
those present, or to its implementation when consensus has
been secured. But Horton didn't really have that option – the
degree of change and the sheer weight of management led him
to choose the more public format.

All change

After Project 1990 had been unveiled and vigorously discussed
at the Compleat Angler, Horton established a Culture Change
Team. Kate Owen was drafted onto this team which was given
the brief to help implement the change process; it had three
months in which to prepare its ground.

'Many companies start a culture change programme', says
Kate Owen, 'many fewer complete it.' Owen admits that they
were unable to complete a comprehensive plan from the
outset. 'It is impossible to design a blueprint for a change
programme on this scale and in a company of this size', she

says today. Having discovered that there was little experience in Britain on which to draw, BP decided to implement the programme largely through its own resources, calling on only a small number of outside advisers and consultants.

Kate Owen's background comprised training and human resources disciplines – her approach to the business of communication is similar to others with a personnel background as we reported in Chapter 2, with a healthy cynicism for 'corporate videos' and a strong emphasis on empowering managers to pass the message to their own staff. The communications professionals on the team provided expertise and the necessary media, but didn't themselves communicate directly with staff.

Three months after the Compleat Angler seminar and one week after Robert Horton took over the chairmanship of BP, Project 1990 was unveiled to BP's staff around the world. David Pascall, who had led the Project 1990 group, and Ian Howell were given the task of travelling the world and launching the new approach. Howell had spent part of his BP career in Public Affairs and is familiar with the 'tools of the trade'; the two men were supported by a kit of slides and booklets which spelled out the principles of Project 1990. Between them they held 50 briefing sessions, attended by groups of varying sizes, the largest being 1,000 at each of four sessions held at BP's American headquarters at Cleveland. In all cases local managers were present to take part and where possible to lead the discussions. In some cases it was the line managers who facilitated the whole session. From then on it was to be the responsibility of managers to communicate and execute, even interpret, the mandate.

The Culture Change Team set itself the target of engaging the Group's top 300 managers, who were invited to one of 13 highly interactive cross-business seminars, each lasting three days, attended in whole or in part by Robert Horton or his deputy David Simon, as well as the managing directors of the three businesses. The seminars emphasised 'what Project 1990 means to you', encouraging those present to pass the accountability for the change programme downwards to their own staff.

The first of these seminars generated a great deal of discussion concerning the new philosophy; by the later meetings the content of Project 1990 had already become familiar and was starting to be implemented locally – so these groups tended to review progress and provide feedback, with fresh emphasis on management action.

Each of BP's businesses – Exploration, Oil and Chemicals – arranged its own change workshops, for which it selected and trained facilitators to support the line managers in running the groups. Eighty per cent of the Group's staff attended some form of change workshop.

'We began to realise what we had unleashed', relates Kate Owen. 'People who hadn't yet attended a change workshop were asking when they were going to get theirs. We couldn't have stopped the process even if we had wanted to.'

Empowerment rules OK

The Head of Human Resources at BP, Richard Newton, gave a talk in March 1993 to an *Economist* conference on empowerment. He spelt out four basic rules for making empowerment effective:

- 'The first is the need to articulate clearly and openly the Company's business goals, both in the short term and of a more visionary nature. There must be a strong emphasis on face-to-face communication at every level. This takes time – management time, and time before the message sinks in and people really understand the business situation. But there are no short cuts. If you want people to rise to the challenges that empowerment presents they must have a good knowledge and understanding of the issues their business faces.'
- 'The second rule is to align individual aspirations with those of the company; in other words, to reconcile career and personal objectives within business goals. Effectively answering the question "If I deliver the performance the

company wants, what's in it for me?" This is the most challenging aspect of the whole empowerment process. How do you tailor reward, recognition and development opportunities to encourage superior performance?

'We describe this as the "yellow brick road" in which an individual's personal journey follows the same path as that of the business. But at some stage along the road there can be a parting of the ways. This need not be something to be feared – indeed, all the training, self-development opportunities and rewards given to individuals in the past may increase their options outside the company.'

- 'The third rule is to recognise, and encourage, business flexibility or diversity. What works in Aberdeen won't necessarily work in Baglan Bay, still less Baku, Bogota or Singapore. The watchword must be "fit for purpose" with decisions taken as close to the local situation as possible.'

- 'That's what I mean by a "learning company" and it's connected with my fourth empowerment rule. If an organisation is to learn from its experiences it must have effective global linkages in place. Those linkages need not necessarily be of policy but will also be of processes, networks – both formal and informal – and behaviour.

'Empowerment can be a great force for liberation – for enabling people to do things better, and to tackle things in totally new ways. But it needs also to be a force for discipline, otherwise what starts out as a democracy may end up in anarchy. There can be a dark side, which must be kept in check. Empowerment is about saying "These are the business goals; these are the targets which must be met; this is the context and these are the processes within which we must operate. Use your own ingenuity, enterprise and initiative in achieving them." '

The process is inexorable; an organisation can start by enrolling its owners to communicate a change message and end up by changing its whole management style. Project 1990 led to formal changes in management techniques; process objectives took their place alongside business objectives, teams were encouraged to devise new ways of measuring performance, based on degrees of improvement rather than quantified financial results. Upward feedback was introduced with what Kate Owen describes as a dramatic change in style; 'In the past, the more senior the manager was, the more likely he was to say that he didn't need formal training. It was enough to attend industry conferences in sunny resorts, hob-nobbing with world leaders. Now, senior managers are genuinely committed to staff development, including their own.'

Charles Nicholson, of BP's Communications Team, tells the recent story of one manager who had 12 people reporting to him; he needed to decide how the year's bonus should be divided among them. Applying the new philosophy, he decided to ask the group for their recommendations. To his surprise, the unanimous view of his staff was that two people should receive the maximum bonus; these were the very people to whom, left to himself, he would have allocated the minimum figure. It emerged that he had underestimated the pair simply because they tended to remain quiet in group discussions; their colleagues knew how great a part they really played.

Teamwork rules. The old days of technical cliques, each working in different blocks isolated from people with different disciplines, now made way for a co-operative approach. In the same way, the teams which had been established to implement the change programme found that they were being metamorphosed into the bloodstream of the company's businesses. Suppliers, too, were offered new relationships, including a share of the profitability of the operations to which they contributed.

Ian Howell underlines the part played in this transformation by face-to-face communication. In the past, there had been excessive reliance on formal communications, via employee publications and videos. Now, the emphasis was on enabling managers to take the lead and speak directly to their staff.

BP probably would not have chosen to tell the Project 1990

story in the strict context of a communications exercise; to Howell and Owen the success of the culture change is more to do with empowerment and teamwork as basic management disciplines and little to do with the contribution of specialist communications specialists. The fact is that BP alone among the major organisations we have encountered has succeeded in 'enrolling its owners' to the point where they facilitate (our term, not BP's!) the process of communicating the company's messages in the fullest sense of that word.

Simon says

'When Horton came in there was in fact no crisis at BP,' says Ian Howell. 'The crisis came two years later with the economic recession and a decline in BP's economic performance. Project 1990 was to do with releasing people to realise their full potential.' When the 1992 crisis came, large numbers of staff were shed. 'The march turned out to be longer and tougher than anyone had anticipated', comments Owen, 'It is doubtful whether we could have survived the recession as well as we did without Project 1990.'

Alongside the recession came Horton's sudden departure from BP in a boardroom coup unprecedented in the company's history. He was succeeded as Chief Executive by his deputy David Simon and, in theory, Project 1990 could have died or at least paused in its tracks, as happened when Crispin Evans left United Distillers at a similar stage in the introduction of a new corporate philosophy (see Chapter 4). In fact, David Simon embraced the concept of 'empowerment' – he admitted he had disliked the word but said that he now understood what it really meant. He described Project 1990 as the best thing Robert Horton did for BP and declared that BP's priority must be to build on the principles established by Project 1990. Better teamwork, he believed, would be the key to restoring the company's performance and reputation.

'Bold strokes, long marches.' David Simon set ambitious

financial targets for the next three years, the so-called '1–2–5' formula: the group was to achieve $1 billion of debt repayment, $2 billion profits and $5 billion capital expenditure a year by 1995; in fact, BP passed all its targets in the previous year; the groundwork laid by Project 1990 was the foundation for this success.

During the worst years of the recession the number of people in the company was halved in the space of just five years; the fight for survival produced a crisis mentality. Inevitably, such dramatic changes have taken their toll; 'Very recently the aim was simply survival,' says Ian Howell, 'Now we are knocked into shape, the aim must be to inspire and motivate people in a way which rekindles their enthusiasm. We have to build a greater sense of perspective, of where we are heading.'

In 1995, John Browne took over from David Simon the post of Chief Executive; he adds his own commentary to the culture change: 'it's about *liking* running marathons,' he said. The first rush of excitement and enthusiasm – the bold strokes – are now in the past. It really is a long march.

What BP teaches us

People in smaller companies may be envious of the resources which a corporate giant can muster; not many of us have the option of sending a change management team off to meet Jack Welch and Rosbeth Moss Kanter; we probably don't have a company cinema in which to hold presentations. However, BP's success in achieving teamwork and empowerment would have been less of a challenge in a smaller organisation. The larger the population of managers, the harder it is to instil a culture of facilitation and the greater BP's achievement in doing so.

The lessons to be learned from the BP study are probably these:

• Build understanding and ownership at all levels and involve as many people as possible in the process of implementing change – enrol your owners.

- Culture change is a long road – a marathon, not a sprint.

There are other aspects of Project 1990 which have not been fully reported here but which underpin the lessons which emerge from other case studies in this book:

- Encourage feedback and the bench-marking of progress.
- Link desired changes in behaviour to business goals.

Finally, the BP case study throws up an interesting perspective on the role of the communications department. Ian Howell spent a period of his BP career as a corporate affairs specialist; Kate Owen's background lies in human resources.

Both believe that communications is first and foremost the responsibility of line management, with the communications specialist playing an important support role – a topic which is currently under review at BP's head office.

In the next case study, we tackle an organisation typical of many process and manufacturing companies. At plant level, people work in a number of shifts, usually alone or in small groups; they do not normally attend meetings. At shop-floor level, interest in the company's philosophy is pretty basic – What does it mean to me? Is my job threatened? Will it affect my wage packet?

Communicating with manual workers is tougher than with office staff; the motivation is less, the practicalities harder to arrange. Furthermore, Courtaulds had the challenge of relaying an important message not only to its British staff but also to workforces in Germany and Spain.

Courtaulds European Fibres – Three into one must go

In 1993, Courtaulds and Hoechst agreed to merge their European Viscose and Acrylic Fibres operations. Three countries were involved: Germany, where the joint venture would take responsibility for Hoechst's factory at Kelheim in Bavaria; Spain, where Courtaulds has a factory in Barcelona; and England, where Courtaulds operates Courtelle and Viscose plants in Grimsby and Westcroft near Bradford. The marketing team is based in Coventry.

The logic behind the merger was impeccable. Hoechst, for its part, wanted to concentrate on its core markets and the Kelheim factory was marginal to that strategy. Courtaulds and Hoechst had been competing in market-places where neither could afford a truly European salesforce; by combining they could market better at lower costs whilst reducing the production costs inherent in rival products.

Chief Executive of the new joint venture was to be Patrick White, an experienced production manager who had just completed a stint at Courtaulds head office in London as Director of Human Resources. In forming the joint venture, both disciplines would be stretched to the full.

National attitudes

Nothing illustrates better the challenge faced by the new company than the difference between the attitudes held in each country towards employee communications. In Germany, communications centred on monthly meetings with representatives of the Works Council, who guarded their prerogative as the route through which management should communicate with its workforce any information relating to terms and conditions. Deprived of direct management channels, the company did from time to time use video with printed booklets to report on performance; this was particularly effective in reaching shift workers, providing the video was kept short and the message stood alone.

The German workforce was unfamiliar with the logic of the merger and was uneasy. The people at Kelheim knew they were the most highly paid in the new joint venture, without offering productivity to match; they felt threatened by lower wages and more cost-effective workforces in Spain and England.

Spain suffered the problems inherent in any factory where people work in small groups and in shift patterns. It was a problem getting sufficient people together away from the line for long enough to conduct cell briefings. Supervisors and foremen had little experience in communicating. The company had introduced new techniques for training personnel to work with the new computerised equipment but it had proved difficult to muster people to take part in the training.

Traditionally, it had been left to the managing director to talk to the troops. They had tried recording his message on videos which were then played in the canteen during meals, but people began to laugh when they saw the same sequences coming round for the second time. The Barcelona plant now convenes a large-scale meeting once a quarter at which the charismatic MD explains in person (with much waving of his arms) how the company is doing. For the rest, the company newsletter is the most important and effective means of reaching the operatives scattered amongst the machinery. Spanish attitudes to the merger were neutral; it all seemed very remote to the Barcelona worker who thought it was unlikely that the joint venture would have much effect on his job or his pay.

Communications were better established at the Grimsby plant. A survey conducted a year previously into employee opinions in both Courtelle and Viscose had demonstrated that the company was not regarded by its staff as effective in communicating. Courtaulds had responded by introducing a new briefing system which now appeared to be working well.

The Grimsby plant faced the same problem as Barcelona, with people working in small groups and shift patterns. The workforce had faced a period of uncertainty just a few years before when Courtaulds had announced that one of its four fibres plant was to be closed – and Grimsby had been favourite. A concerted campaign had saved the plant on that occasion, but the viscose fibres staff now felt threatened by the invest-

ment which the company was making in its new product,
Tencel, at that time manufactured only in America and
seemingly the blue-eyed favourite in the battle for company
money and resources.

None the less, the company was communicating well with its
staff at Grimsby and Westcroft thanks to a system of cell
briefings which were held once a month for 10 to 15 minutes,
short enough not to damage productivity. It faced, however,
the same problem as Barcelona, namely the lack of skills at
supervisor level in facilitating these sessions.

Communication was less of a problem at the sales and
marketing end of Courtaulds UK, based in Coventry. This unit
is relatively small and, through the nature of its work, familiar
with the market-place served by both Hoechst and Courtaulds;
they could understand the logic of the merger. They were also
familiar with the media of communication.

Merger mania

Not only had both Courtaulds and Hoechst admitted to
weaknesses in employee communications but Patrick White
now faced the obstacles inherent in all mergers and take-overs.
Any company which has gone through the process will recognise
the stages. First comes a period during which the negotiations
take place in secret, when rumours often begin to circulate. This
is followed by a further period when the news is out but when
the negotiations are far from complete. Managers are tied into
seemingly endless meetings with lawyers and accountants and
there is no firm information with which to reassure the troops.
This doesn't hamper the newspapers and the investment
community who purport to know everything that is going on –
and what they don't know they freely embellish, to the growing
disquiet of the people on the shop floor.

Next comes a frantic period during which the management
teams from each corner meet and get to know each other; they
must quickly become familiar with operations which were

previously sworn rivals. All the while, uncertainty is eating at the new relationships; the rationale behind any merger is rationalisation – is your job on the line or is mine?

A queue forms of groups who must be briefed and reassured that the merger will not harm them. Any company will move first to reassure the clients on whom its business depends, followed by the investment community which can mark the company's value up or down according to their mood. Whilst the salesforce frantically soothe the major clients and head office reassures the City, the workforce hasn't actually been forgotten, it just takes time before the management can tell them anything definite, and a lot of time before they will hear the most important message of all, 'your job is safe'.

The communications process

Into this cauldron of languages, cultures and staff attitudes, the Courtaulds/Hoechst joint venture team faced the challenge of explaining to staff in all three countries why the merger was taking place and what effect it would have on each plant and its staff. In the breakneck haste with which this merger was negotiated and concluded it is to the credit of Courtaulds that thought had been given at the earliest stage to employee communications. One of Patrick White's first acts had been to assemble a communications working party with representatives from each country. The Human Resources Director for Courtaulds Fibres Ltd, Terry Keeling, was given responsibility for co-ordinating and rolling out the message.

Even when Courtaulds and Hoechst were still locked into detailed negotiations, White was determined to keep staff briefed at every stage. The joint venture didn't have at its disposal the kind of money and resources which other companies in this book were able to command; indeed, it would have alienated the staff if it had been seen to squander money on conspicuous communications. On the other hand, with the management team preoccupied with devising new strategies and implementing new policies, White and Keeling knew that they needed help from the outside.

A key player in formulating the new strategy of the joint venture had been Stewart Timperley, a professor from the London Business School (LBS). He was on a year's sabbatical from LBS and had worked closely with Patrick White throughout the planning stages. In March 1994, Timperley had helped run a three-day seminar for the senior managers of the three nations which had given White his first opportunity to spell out his strategy and for the new management team to get to know each other and discuss how they would work together.

Thanks to this groundwork one of the key requirements for effective communications had been achieved early in the process – the strategy was clearly stated. Workhouse's first meeting with Patrick White and Stewart Timperley was held in April 1994. White tabled a short list of requirements for the communications campaign – a model briefing:

Objectives
- 'Raise awareness internally of the various issues facing the joint venture, standards, improve motivation.'
- 'Develop a communications plan for all employees linked to the launch and any supporting events.'

Key areas
- Explain the rationale for the joint venture.
- Provide appropriate information on the capabilities of the joint venture.
- Establish appropriate expectations.
- Break down language and cultural barriers.
- Core areas plus local flexibility.
- Be proactive in creating discussion and action in each unit.

Success criteria
- Ready to go by early June.
- Achieve the communications standards of the business appropriate to 'Investors in People'.

- Speed up both local improvements in performance and development of synergy.
- Instil sense of pride within the employees.

The media kit

Courtaulds readily agreed to a mixed media approach. The subject was too complex to be covered in any one medium, least of all a single video programme. Each aspect of the joint venture would throw up a number of issues which staff would want to challenge and discuss – the message must therefore be broken down into topics which could be debated separately. Each of the sites would require detailed information relevant to German, Spanish or British staff; some sections must therefore be tailored to local needs.

It was agreed that Patrick White should appear on video talking about the aims of the Courtaulds/Hoechst joint venture, while Stewart Timperley would give the broader picture of the logic behind the merger. The video would be divided into four modules, each supported by slides. A briefing pack would be prepared for the facilitators at each site; this provided suggestions for running the groups and contained printed detail to provide background information for the facilitators in case the discussion should stray beyond the subject matter contained in the video and the slides.

The video modules would in turn describe the background to a topic and tee up a question for the group to address. The first module provided a general background to the three companies and the logic behind the merger. Patrick White says:

> We've got three companies, they are all small regional players, they are successful in their own right but we believe that by putting them together we can really play to their strengths . . .

while Stewart Timperley paints the broader picture:

> You will see in the next few years a major transformation
> of large German companies . . . focusing on core busi-
> nesses, playing particular attention to your resource avail-
> ability . . . you can't do everything and for Hoechst it is a
> question of focusing on their core areas.

When the video module had been seen, the manager facilitating the session would put up a slide which posed a blunt
question – 'Do you agree with Patrick White's assessment of
the benefits of the joint venture?'; the facilitator then invited
the group to debate the issues raised in the video so far.

The second sequence addresses the markets which the joint
venture will serve and the products with which it will attack
these markets. Stewart Timperley points out that the merged
companies:

> . . . would severely threaten Lenzing on the viscose side
> . . . the market share of the two businesses put together
> would severely threaten Enichem. From the market share
> growth standpoint, there is a lot of sense in the market
> position of the new joint venture.

Followed by Patrick White with a clear strategy statement:

> Our objectives are to take those good products, to make
> certain that our whole commercial team fully appreciate
> *where* we are really good and get them to identify the
> customers where those products will really be appreciated
> . . . we want to be supplying those customers which are
> going to be successful, not those customers which might
> fade away.

The module then presents the joint venture's strategy for
production. Patrick White again . . .

> The joint venture provides us with an opportunity to sell
> the products we are best at in each unit right across
> Europe . . . If you view it from the customer's point of
> view, that means one-stop shopping – he would be able to
> buy all of his requirements from us.

The module ends by challenging staff to identify the best and the worst products made in their unit – a question designed to send a chill down the spine of people working on the less successful lines.

The third module deals with productivity and technology and in particular with research and development.

> All four manufacturing centres in the joint venture have made impressive progress in R&D, to improve both the quality of their products and the levels of productivity. Bringing together these pools offers a real opportunity for the businesses to learn from each other and help spread the burden of R&D across the joint venture.

Patrick White then threw down another challenge:

> In the Far East the new factories are producing 200 tonnes of fibre for every employee every year. Now we have set an internal target in Europe of 150 tonnes. Now that has to be a short-term target and we have to see the benefits of the joint venture help us rapidly to get up towards that 200 level.

These figures were worrying to workforces, not all of which – notably Kelheim – were achieving 150 tonnes a year. The module ends with another question: 'How would your plant benefit from specialising in selected products?' By now, even those who thought that the joint venture would have little effect on their operation would have woken up to the need for a startling increase in productivity to match competitors in South-East Asia, and the fear that some lines would be closed down or, at the very least, adapted to new products.

The final module addresses values and standards – the all-important issue of the new joint venture's corporate philosophy, how staff are expected to behave in the new operations. Patrick White:

> The real goal is . . . everybody being champions of their own business yet wanting to do the right thing for the joint

venture. That really means people sticking with the
culture that they know best, operating in the way that they
know best, yet being prepared to learn and adapt from
other values, so that we get the best of both worlds.

This was followed by the final question: 'How can we speed up
the necessary process of change?'

In other words, the media kit pulled no punches. Patrick
White's statements were brief and clear. The logic behind the
merger dictated a review of the businesses to establish which
unit was providing the market with products it wanted at prices
which matched the opposition. Each site would be asked to
research and produce those chemicals with which it performed
better than the other plants in the joint venture. Those which
were doing less well than their opposite numbers would be
made aware of the need to improve performance or even
change their products.

Piloting the package

Courtaulds recognised that the message needed careful handling
if it were not to demotivate or confuse its audience. Despite the
shortage of time, a period was set aside for piloting the media.
Late in May, Terry Keeling assembled a group of managers
from all the UK plants and offices to view a rough edit of the
video and drafts of the slides. Reactions were a mixture of the
pragmatic and the defiant.

A number of small points were dealt with. The meeting was
delayed while technicians tried to locate a 35-millimetre slide
projector – at which point the group put forward its first
recommendation, that slides should be replaced by acetates
since overhead projectors were more readily available at most
sites. When it viewed the video modules the group felt that the
trigger questions should be adapted to each audience; they
should therefore not be imprinted on the video, as originally
planned, but projected on slides.

The first module proved useful in giving background information but was too general to stimulate specific discussion points – it would be better for the facilitator to use this break to provide local information at plant level.

The main debate centred on the level of information which could be released to staff. How would R&D staff react to the clear message that they might lose work to their rivals? Would shift workers really want to be involved in discussion of markets and philosophies? Wasn't it dangerous to unleash such profound questions about their future before clear answers could be given?

After this session, Workhouse and Courtaulds worked together to amend video, text and overheads; a few days later the whole pack was available in all three languages. Then Terry Keeling and his fellow managers rolled their sleeves up and set out to communicate the joint venture message.

The first hundred days

Three months later, Terry Keeling took stock of the effects of the roll-out. He described the joint venture as, now, 'three separate independent companies which are now well aware of each other. They are aware that there will need to be some change, but most people believe that it probably won't affect them. Generally speaking, the change has affected the organis-ation rather than the individual units.' In other words, a successful outcome considering the degree of trauma which normally accompanies a major merger of this kind.

Keeling reports that each unit continues to carry a different perception of the joint venture, that they still carry different agendas dating from their previous existences. Kelheim has suffered the most anxiety. Its staff know that they cost more than their opposite numbers in Spain and Britain without the productivity to justify that cost; their anxiety, however, doesn't date from the formation of the joint venture. They had been uncomfortably aware that Hoechst was disenchanted by its profitability; if anything, the merger with Courtaulds has

given them hope rather than fear. The communications programme has, however, brought home to the staff and management at Kelheim the extent to which other companies are more
competitive and reinforced their perception that change is
inevitable.

Spain continues to feel 'untainted' by the merger, that there
will be no material change in its situation. Meanwhile, says
Keeling, 'the UK factories have grown more aware of the
potential for the future, a significant change from the recent
past when the Grimsby plant had only narrowly escaped
closure. The UK plants had never opposed the merger, as
Spain had done, and are now firmly convinced that Courtaulds
is committed to the Fibres business.'

Each site had conducted its communications exercise in
different ways and on different time-scales. The UK had been
able to move most quickly, for two reasons. Firstly, it had a
well-established pattern of team and cell briefings which was
easily adapted to this roll-out. Secondly, all the managers who
had attended the screening of the pilot materials now acted as
facilitators, for example, John Farmer, the Production Director,
ran sessions for hundreds of his people, while at the other end
of the scale, David Powers, the Commercial Director, facilitated six or so screenings.

In Germany and Spain the cascade was conducted exclusively
by the two representatives of each country who attended the
Communications Committee, Gerhardt Schafer and Geza
Hidazi in Kelheim and Jesus Palacios and Fernando Senar in
Spain. Inevitably, it took them longer to hold all the necessary
briefings. (Interestingly, the Kelheim managers found the
cascade process useful in establishing a direct link with their
workforce, bypassing for once the all-powerful Works Councils).

Keeling speaks highly of the video modules and the part they
played in the process. The feedback particularly from the
English workforce emphasised the sharp focus which the
videos placed on the joint venture, thanks in large part to
Patrick White's contribution. VHS had been found to be a
flexible medium; thanks to the abundance of training units

there had been no difficulty finding viewing facilities. The response had come in a variety of shades:

> At one end of the spectrum, the response was bland – they thanked us for taking the time and trouble to explain the joint venture but had few questions to ask. At another end, staff had subjected their managers to a lively debate, asking good questions and raising interesting points. One couldn't describe the whole exercise as the answer to a maiden's prayer – they didn't contribute a host of bright ideas or anything. But everyone does now know what the joint venture is about.

It is important to Terry Keeling that communication doesn't stop with the first exercise. He doesn't, however, feel that Courtaulds European Fibres is likely to establish a regular pattern of programmes on the grand scale: 'We have our monthly team briefings which are successful in passing routine information all the way down the company. To repeat the scale of this introductory programme we would need something meaty to report. Perhaps the first full year's figures.'

Most importantly, all the objectives set by Patrick White in his briefing document had been achieved. Almost uniquely among the projects reported in this book, a communications project had been fully plotted, planned, conducted and measured against its original targets.

Lessons from the Courtaulds case study

The briefing given by Patrick White was a model of its kind; it set clear targets making it possible to measure performance. The rule book on which this chapter is based spells out the importance in any communications project of establishing measurable goals.

One ingredient in Courtaulds' success – at least in the Grimsby plant – lay in the existence of a pattern of cell briefings. All too often, organisations attempt to communicate important messages to all members of the workforce where there is no foundation to build on; it is hardly surprising when the system creaks and collapses. Managers who have no experience of briefing their staff cannot be expected suddenly to develop presentation skills; the necessary equipment won't be to hand and, worst of all, staff will approach the first-time roll-out with a degree of cynicism.

Courtaulds set aside enough time and resources. Despite the pressures of negotiating the joint venture, the schedule allowed for the videos to be piloted in the presence of the managers who would be responsible for presenting them. Their views were noted and at least a dozen amendments were made to the video modules; the text of the handbooks was similarly adjusted.

Placing Patrick White's statements firmly on the record, on video, was an important step in reducing confusion; we shall see another example of this in the next case study.

At the time of writing, there are some wrinkles to be ironed out. At Kelheim, the roll-out has taken longer than planned largely because there was no tradition of management communication on this scale. The Spanish workforce still regards the joint venture as a distant phenomenon which will not affect them. Courtaulds has yet to decide what should be the next stage in the process, with the inevitable danger that there might be no next stage and consequently no 'long march' to follow the 'bold stroke'.

However, in Keeling's view, the communication succeeded in conveying a complex message to the most challenging of all business audiences, the shop-floor workers of a manufacturing plant. Furthermore, the whole exercise was conducted on a small budget and gave good value for money, as did the subject of our next study.

Meridian – The new age of broadcasting

On 16 October 1993, the chief executive of Meridian Broadcasting, Roger Laughton, received a momentous fax. It had been despatched by the Independent Television Commission, along with over 40 other faxes announcing the results of the 'Great ITV Franchise Auction'. It told Meridian that it had won the franchise, previously operated by Television South, to broadcast in the South and South-east of England – the most prosperous region, along with London, in the ITV network.

At the time Meridian had fewer than 10 people on the full-time payroll. Fourteen months later the company was to be 'on air' and there would be well over 300 staff. It now faced the challenge of recruiting these people, buying or building its broadcast facilities, training the people to operate the equipment, and – almost as a by-product – of introducing a radically new philosophy to the ITV system.

Like Carlton, which had been successful in winning the weekday London franchise, Meridian planned to operate as a publisher/broadcaster. This label was new to the British broadcasting vocabulary; it meant that the new companies would operate in a manner quite unlike the established ITV companies – the so-called producer/broadcasters, which employ large teams of programme makers to produce almost all the programmes they broadcast. The new contractors were to commission their programmes from the new and growing breed of independent producers. Carlton was to go even further than Meridian and commission its news programmes from outside; Meridian would produce its own news programme from centres in Southampton, Maidstone and Newbury. It would also make its 'community' programmes in-house; the rest would be made outside.

The new philosophy was enshrined in the company's Mission Statement, which itself had been part of its application to the ITC:

> Meridian will build a successful long-term broadcasting business in the South and South East:
>
> • by providing a service of exceptional quality
> • by providing a service of exceptional value for money

- by publishing programmes for Channel 3 which reflect the tastes and interests of our viewers
- by playing a full part in the management of Channel 3 so that the region's interests are fully reflected in each aspect of its operations.

This new way of working was anathema to the people who had worked for TVS, 200 of whom were now recruited into Meridian. It presented less of a challenge to the others, many of whom came from radio and from outside the world of broadcasting and who faced a different challenge, that of adapting to a television culture. So Meridian faced a double hurdle in the short time available – it had to devise and introduce radically new ways of working; it had also to blend together a diverse group of people, some demoralised and resentful at the collapse of TVS and other companies, others facing a completely new working environment.

Its approach was typical of the company – brisk, determined, no-nonsense. Firstly, it identified a project team to supervise the process. This was headed by Keith Clement, an immensely experienced programme executive who had managed to time his arrival at Meridian to follow directly after the party which the BBC had staged to mark his retirement after 35 years' service. The Human Resources and Training Executives of the new company also joined the group, along with Peter Booth, the Director of Engineering.

The team decided to stage a number of half-day seminars, to which all members of staff would be invited (most of them before they officially joined the company – and in their own time!). Fourteen were held in all, in hotel conference rooms near the three new television centres. The sessions were divided into five sections and run to a strict timetable:

Timetable
09.00–09.45   Introduction to Meridian Broadcasting
09.45–10.30   Network and Regional Feature Programmes
10.30–10.45   Coffee Break

10.45–11.15   Regional News Centres
11.15–12.00   Human Resource Development and Training
12.00–12.45   Conditions of Service
12.45–13.00   Public Affairs

Each section was built around a video sequence comprising, for the most part, interviews with Roger Laughton and a small number of senior staff. Slides were used to illustrate a variety of complex issues, from the regional layout of the new operation to the marketing profile of the television audience.

The whole exercise was built around the Mission Statement which appeared firstly in bullet point form in the video and again in summary on slides which were left on the screen during discussion. The fist video module featured the chief executive Roger Laughton adding a commentary to the bare bones of the Statement:

> It is in our interest to provide programmes of quality because that's the way we shall build ratings and that's the way we'll build revenue.

He went on to describe the difference between the old world of the broadcaster/producer, in which the ITV stations made their own programmes, and the new regime of the publisher/broadcaster, in which a large number of the programmes would be commissioned from independent producers:

> Meridian has to differentiate its broadcasting activity from its publishing activity . . .

and Laughton made a bold prophecy:

> I predict that there will be no so-called producer/broadcasters in five years' time.

He launched the first discussion with a challenge:

> We start in the knowledge that we're going straight into

1993 and a different kind of competitive world from the
one we've grown up in.

The facilitator then invited discussion; possible topics for
debate were suggested in the facilitators' notes:

- Revenue is returning slowly to the ITV system.
- We will be trying to maintain our audiences – but so will our
  competitors.
- We shall have real competition for commercial audiences for
  the first time. Programme schedules are crucial because
  advertisers want to reach as many of their target purchasers
  as possible.
- Revenue success will be related to audience success.
- The Meridian objective is to maximise revenue, therefore
  viewer appeal to the channel is essential.

In brief, these points summarise the harsh world of independent
television as it emerged from the recession of the early 1990s into
the new competitive environment of satellite-delivered programmes and computer-based entertainment. In the struggle
to stop revenues falling, there would be no prisoners –
neighbouring ITV stations would be as eager to pick up over-
lap audiences and advertisers as the BBC to retain its viewers
and BSkyB to win them from all terrestrial broadcasters. Even
Channel Four, previously planned in close collaboration with
ITV, would be entering the battle with gusto!

The second session concentrated on the programming philosophy which the new station would adopt. Here, wisely, the
policy would be 'steady as she goes'. Meridian's predecessor,
TVS, had arrived on the scene a decade earlier with a 'new-
broom' policy which had proved seriously unpopular with the
mainly conservative viewers in the South. In the second video
module Mary McAnally, Meridian's Controller of Regional
Features, underlined the need for continuity:

Our plans for regional programmes are to build on the
strong legacy left behind by TVS.

Unlike the so-called network companies – the big five stations based in London, Birmingham, Manchester and Leeds – it was the prime responsibility of the other 10 stations to serve their own regions, as Roger Laughton spelled out:

> Regional programmes are a prime condition of our licence with the ITC [Independent Television Commission]. The network programmes are an aspiration.

It is a fact of commercial broadcasting that regional companies in the ITV system make the most profits when they stick to their own patch and avoid the expense of making the kind of big-name dramas and entertainment shows which are seen as the responsibility of Carlton, Central, LWT, Granada and Yorkshire. Most people working in television want to see their programmes shown on the network; Meridian, sensibly, was making it clear from the outset that this was not the reason for which it had been granted the franchise – it would be judged by the quality of its regional output.

Finally, Laughton spelled out Meridian's policy towards its independent suppliers. Like Marks and Spencer, it wanted to ensure the quality and health of its core contractors:

> We should get stability of supply through developing relationships with a relatively small number of independents rather than with every independent.

During the coffee break the audience were given an 'ice-breaking' task, that of devising a title for the nightly news magazine programme which Meridian would produce out of its three centres. (The unimaginative title which was finally chosen – 'Meridian Tonight' – was in fact the most frequently suggested – perhaps the first example of industrial democracy producing the name of a core series.)

The next session started with a guided tour of the map of the Meridian region complete with an explanation of the way in which the new broadcasters would divide this into three sub-regions, with a new centre in Newbury to serve the north Hampshire and Berkshire audiences which had long felt remote from the news programmes generated in Southampton. The third video module showed work taking place on the Newbury studio, which was being hastily constructed in a standard industrial unit on a distinctly unglamorous business estate, a far cry from the days of ostentatious television centres occupying prime sites in city centres.

Next came human resources and terms and conditions of employment – the nitty-gritty of the day. All staff had been sent in advance a copy of the terms and conditions on offer by the company – themselves a shock to graduates from the old world of independent television. In the past, expense allowances had been generous: a machiavellian bundle of no-meal-break payments, double bubbles, first-class travel and generous hospitality allowances. The gravy train was now pushed firmly into a siding, to make way for tough rules which applied from bottom to top of the company.

'There's no point in us demanding value for money performance', said Director of Public Affairs Simon Albury, in his video interview, 'if we are not ourselves leading a value for money existence. Roger Laughton is the Mahatma Gandhi of television . . .' a description borne out by the fact that, unlike his TVS predecessor, there was to be no chauffeur-driven car to waft him between locations – instead, he claimed to be the only ITV chief executive who travelled on the District Line.

It was a nostalgic commission for Workhouse to produce the media package. Michael Blakstad had been Director of Programmes for TVS when it had won the franchise back in 1980; he had lived through the uncomfortable process of taking staff over from the previous contractor – Southern Television – and persuading them to change allegiance to a small group of senior managers imposed on them by the Independent Broadcasting Authority (as the ITC then was). Workhouse itself produces television programmes – it had signed up to the Meridian bid and had joined in the celebrations when its chosen ally had won the auction. It also understood just how controversial some of the new proposals would be.

Laughton himself attended some of the seminars, to answer

questions and join in the discussion. He didn't take the opportunity to deliver the message in person in place of screening the videos, for a very important reason: 'All members of the course had to receive the same consistent message,' he said, 'particularly when it came to principles of employment and conditions of service.'

The point is important. The process of producing media is in itself a distillation of the truth; it forces the participants to finalise their policy and sign it off. A television background helps; in driving the interview home and refusing to accept jargon or half-truths, the interviewer forces the company's executives to focus their corporate philosophy. It can be a painful process for people used to hiding behind management-speak or lengthy qualifying clauses. The fact that Laughton and the other executives were themselves graduates of the television business helped achieve succinct and articulate statements – part of the process of 'putting it on the record'.

The other reason why Meridian insisted on showing the video clips even when the interviewees were present at the seminar was the simple fact that no one could then argue about *what* had been said (however much they might disagree with the statements). It's not only the audience who can mis-remember what was said – very often the speaker inadvertently misses out a key phrase or strays from the text and can't remember afterwards just what he or she had or hadn't said. Video can be spooled back and played again – humans can't.

A by-product of the video route was the opportunity, as Laughton put it 'for everyone to meet most of the senior people in the company' – doubly important since the 350 staff would be working in centres scattered around the South, South East and London, with their executives ricocheting around the region.

Meridian reckons that the modular design of the course made it possible for different groups of Meridian executives to run it. In practice, the same small group who had devised the course ran the seminars – Keith Clement and Peter Booth, along with Human Resources Director Fiona Makowski and

Training Manager Ed Boyce. There were, however, occasions when the key people were absent; other executives less familiar with the material found it easy to step into their shoes. 'Also,' says Keith Clement, 'the course could be affected by the audience. If there was a preponderance of news staff, for example, more emphasis could be placed on their interests'. Since all Meridian staff were required to attend, there were often senior people present who were asked to contribute in their particular area and who shared in the answers during the debates at the end of the session.

A survey was conducted of a random sample of those who attended the courses. Reactions varied from a grim appreciation that this was to be a very different employment scene from the gravy train days of ITV – to surprise that a new company, which hadn't even started operations, could be so clearly focused in its intentions.

Three years later, Meridian was operating profitably and hadn't faced any serious problems in introducing the stringent terms and conditions of employment. Its news programmes won the prestigious Royal Television Society award in their first year and the station emerged from the first ITC review in a far better light than the other three newcomers to the ITV scene. It went into profit earlier than expected and in 1994 it took over another, older regional company, Anglia Television. It is doubtful whether all this could have been achieved if staff hadn't been brought on side from the birth – even the conception – of the company.

For its part, Meridian was pleased that it had been able to achieve this level of communication at a total cost (hotel suites, media, executive time) of just £70 a head. As Keith Clement said, '. . . it is difficult to do better than that'.

Lessons from the Meridian case study

There's a saying in the IT business – 'never computerise a moving target'. The same applies in communicating corporate strategies. It is a mistake to attempt to create media and roll-out messages when the story hasn't yet been finalised. Because Meridian had included in its franchise bid a complete Mission Statement, its strategy was already in place. Furthermore, the company had an armoury of articulate executives who could express the Mission with ease and conviction.

What Meridian lacked, in comparison with Courtaulds, say, or BP, was a corps of managers on whom it could draw to facilitate the seminars. Wisely, the company decided to stick with the team which had created the programme and who were familiar with both the message and the media. Furthermore, the performance of this team improved over the period of the 14 introductory sessions; this illustrates the importance of re-hearsal and practice to even the most experienced facilitators.

Finally, Meridian took the opportunity created by its use of media to place its philosophy firmly on the record; there was no arguing about what had been said. When it came to tough messages such as the proposed terms and conditions, the fact that the policy had been carved, as it were, onto master tape meant that there was no possibility of misinterpretation or negotiation.

Checklist

This chapter has featured three case studies which demonstrate the importance of the facilitator in the process of employee communications. The main lessons which can be drawn from them are:

- Identify the facilitators early in the process. Wherever possible, they should have run seminars or focus groups for their people before this programme.
- Prepare clear instructions for the facilitators, preferably in text form.
- Run a pilot session wherever possible, allowing the facilitators to act as guinea pigs; take into account the points they make and adjust the materials accordingly.

- Give the facilitators an opportunity themselves to rehearse the presentation; if training is necessary this should be provided.
- Take as few risks with your facilitators as possible; if in doubt, resort to managers whom you are sure have good presentation skills.
- Allocate enough staff time as is necessary, and ensure that the necessary screening facilities etc are available.

We shall see in the next chapter that facilitators can themselves play an additional role in the cascade process; once they have been briefed and enrolled, they can often become the best possible ambassadors for the strategy.

6

Selecting the Media – Nuclear Electric, Railtrack

Choosing the right media to achieve the most effective communications is a science which is still not well understood by many managers. In Chapter 2 we touched on some of the research that has given indications of which media can be used most effectively for different purposes. However, there are still no clearly agreed paradigms which form the base of the science. In this chapter we will provide some simple guidelines for media selection.

In all communications the determinants for selecting media are what is necessary or what is possible. It should also be remembered that effective communications often require a degree of redundancy of presentation built in to ensure the main message is received, or for reinforcement; there is still some truth in the old saw that the most effective technique is to, 'Tell them what you are going to tell them. Tell them, then tell them what you told them.'

It is often important to present a message on more than one medium to achieve the best result. Sometimes this may mean the selection of a primary medium with a secondary medium for reinforcement. Sometimes it may be important to ensure that the message is directly enhanced by interaction between two or more media. There are six main factors which must affect media selection:

- The nature of the message.
- The nature of the audience.
- Time.
- The communications environment.
- The abilities of the selected communicators and the robustness of the media.
- Cost.

One of the great benefits of any concrete medium: print, audio, video or modern electronic media, is that they can ensure a consistency and clarity of message which reduce reliance upon human communicators to understand, interpret or clearly express complex issues. However, different media are obviously better adapted to different types of message. Print media tend to be better adapted to convey large quantities of detailed information. Audio can be used to pursue arguments and to reinforce particular points. Video can compress information and make clear illustrated points quickly and effectively.

Modern electronic media offer an extraordinary range of possibilities. Electronic mail offers rapid communications via telephone systems and office automation technology (PC and mainframe) to carefully targeted groups. Completely interactive packages of text, voice, graphics and video can be delivered on fixed media such as CD-ROM or via ISDN links or satellite broadcast. These allow the organisation to tailor the message to different groups within the organisation through defining access levels, and also allow the individual to focus on the underlying detail of a particular communication by optional 'drill down'.

The communications environment is also extremely important. The communicator may have the best slides and videos in the world but they will be next to useless if the environment in which they are to be delivered does not have an adequate slide projector or the video monitor is too small to permit all the audience to see the screen. This may sound very obvious but studies have shown that some major UK companies have sent out communications materials to their operating units which are wholly inappropriate for use within the normal working environments. One UK company invested a seven figure sum in developing a major interactive video programme on laser discs for worldwide communications before finding that climatic conditions in many parts of the world caused consistent equipment failure.

The credibility of speakers with their audiences and their basic speaking abilities are clearly very important in carrying out effective communications with a facilitator. The effectiveness of even the very best facilitators can be destroyed if they fumble with the media that are being used to support presentations. It takes a great deal of work to design the best media. It only takes a small failure to neutralise all the good intentions. Too many communicators fall off the cutting edge of presentation technology.

Cost is always an important consideration. There is rarely a unique solution to a communications problem given all the parameters: time-scale, size of audience, locations of audience, complexity of message, audience attitudes, accepted practice, risk factor of failure etc. As with any business decision, the selected solution should be guided by the level of investment that will make most business sense. Within many companies, one can see the classic tendency to overengineer communications with expensive media which do not provide value for money. On the other hand, there are still too many organisations who underestimate the sophistication and believe that communications can always be achieved on the cheap through a combination of Chinese whispers and simple print alone.

The costs of good communications may sometimes be high but the costs of bad communications are even higher. In Chapter 4 we looked at a complex communications programme, United Distillers, which was delivered using a wide variety of media. Distillers selected each medium to meet the needs of a particular aspect of the communications task. Let's now look at two other cases and then try to develop a simple checklist for primary and secondary media selection.

Nuclear Electric – the best ambassadors

Nuclear Electric has known for some time that its best ambassadors are its own people. As often happens in businesses where the product attracts criticism, the staff of Nuclear Electric do a powerful job in arguing the merits of nuclear generation to all and sundry, in the pubs, at community meetings, to anyone who will listen.

Nuclear power stations are mainly located on remote stretches of coastline and for this reason tend to dominate local employment and politics. Because the technology is controversial, but also because the science of nuclear power is fascinating, the company is frequently called upon to defend or simply explain itself to Women's Institutes, to schools, to local councillors and MPs or to people visiting the stations on open days.

For all these reasons, Nuclear Electric works hard to explain itself. It plays a leading role in all the communities in which it is located; each location has an elaborate visitor centre fully equipped with the most modern display technology to describe and explain the nuclear industry – they have become one of the most unlikely tourist successes of the second half of the twentieth century.

In addition, and key to this case study, Nuclear Electric had identified a group of volunteers in each site (including its headquarters and laboratories in Gloucestershire) who are willing and able to speak in public on behalf of the company. The company's highly professional public relations team provides this 'talks service' with slides, videos, literature and up-to-date briefings relevant to the diverse audiences and topics they are called on to address. The existence of this team, and of the culture they represent, played a crucial role when Nuclear Electric was required during 1994 to put its case to government and justify its very existence.

The birth of a company

The company had only been conceived on 9 November 1989, another by-product of the government's volte-face on electricity privatisation. It was thrust into a hostile world with a very short time in which to prove that it could stand on its own two feet.

During the 1980s, the 13 nuclear power stations in England

and Wales had been the responsibility of the Central Electricity Generating Board (CEGB), along with a mixture of coal and oil-fired power stations and some hydroelectric and experimental renewable schemes. Chairman of the CEGB was the brooding, mercurial figure Lord (Walter) Marshall, previously director of Harwell and a passionate advocate of nuclear energy. Marshall was reckoned to be Margaret Thatcher's 'favourite scientist'; she admired his combination of intelligence and power-play.

In early 1989, the government announced its plans to privatise the entire electricity supply industry, lock, stock and reactor. The nuclear stations were to be hived off into the larger of the two new Gencos, then called 'Big G', later to become National Power. Lord Marshall was to be Chairman of this massive enterprise, comprising the majority of the country's fossil-fired stations as well as the 13 nuclear power stations, yet his reaction was one of combined shock and fury. Workhouse produced a video to be shown to the staff of the CEGB in which Nick Ross interviewed the Chairman. Marshall put a brave face on the breaking up of the Board, reflecting that National Power would still be one of the largest companies in Britain, but then allowed his feelings to show. 'I have allowed myself to be shocked and angry for one week,' he said. 'I recommend the staff of the CEGB to do the same – and then get on with the job.'

Things got worse. The City made it clear that National Power would find it hard to attract investment if its portfolio included the nuclear stations. There were a number of reasons for their distrust. Firstly, closer examination of the books of the CEGB revealed that its reporting of the financial perform-ance of the nuclear generators had been seriously muddled; its Board had failed to draw attention to the failure of the new Advanced Gas Cooled Reactors to achieve the levels of output for which they had been designed. Secondly, the Board had re-invested the money which should have been set aside for disposing of radioactive waste and decommissioning nuclear reactors when they reached the end of their operating lives. The process of dismantling an irradiated building is potentially more complex and expensive than building it in the first place; it is certainly less well understood.

Hopes had been raised when, on 5 November that year, Mrs Thatcher made a speech to an international environmental conference in Toronto in which she had praised to the skies the cleanliness of nuclear electricity. These hopes were dashed the following Thursday when the Secretary of State for Energy, John Wakeham, announced in Parliament that the nuclear stations were to be withdrawn from the privatisation of the electricity supply industry. A new public company was to be formed to operate the 13 reactors then functioning in England and Wales and a levy would be established to help cover the costs of waste disposal and decommissioning which had been incurred over 25 years of nuclear operation. Alone in the electricity supply industry, Nuclear Electric would remain in public ownership, its destiny in the hands of the Secretary of State for Energy.

This much had been expected, even if it did dash Lord Marshall's last remaining hopes of retaining control of a giant generating enterprise. However, the government's irritation at what it had found in the CEGB's books was made ominously clear in the next part of the Secretary of State's announcement to the Commons.

The case had been vigorously made by Lord Marshall that the old Magnox stations were approaching the end of their operating lives and would have to be replaced. The future of nuclear electricity in Britain depended on the building of pressurised water reactors (PWRs). The work which had started on Sizewell B was planned as the first construction in a series of four which would be built to identical Westinghouse designs. Wakeham had turned a deaf ear to Marshall's logic; he now announced a moratorium on the building of any PWRs (other than Sizewell B). The moratorium was to last until 1994 when the government would conduct a thorough review of the nuclear industry before considering fresh funding of the PWR programme. It was clear to everyone that this review would seal the future of the industry which, without new stations, would gradually wind itself down as the old stations reached the end of their operating lives. Furious and humiliated, Lord Marshall contemplated resignation.

On the very day that Wakeham made his announcement in the Commons, he summoned to his office the then chairman of the UKAEA, John Collier. Collier had been involved for a couple of months in discussions with the Department of Energy concerning the likely separation of the six Magnox reactors from the privatisation of National Power; it had been mooted that he might share chairmanship of the UKAEA with the same role in a new Magnox company. As Collier describes the mid-morning meeting on 9 November:

> He explained the situation and asked me directly if I would accept the post of Chairman of a new state-owned nuclear generation company. He went on to say that he had to stand up in the House of Commons at 4 pm and that it would be helpful if he could include my name in the statement. I acquiesced. He reminded me that it was only 22 weeks to 'vesting'; he did not want the privatisation delayed. I walked out of the office with no idea of how to form a company let alone have it up and running in 22 weeks.

Over lunch, Collier drew up notices to staff at both organisations – AEA and CEGB – to explain what was happening. He then went to see John Baker, designated to be Chief Executive of National Power. Together with other directors of the CEGB they listened live to Wakeham's announcement. Because of the delicacy of Lord Marshall's position, they agreed to give no press interviews but to issue written statements. Collier relates: 'I was due to go to a symphony concert at the Festival Hall that night. I decided to go and forget the events of the day. Ellen and I got to our flat late evening. I turned on the news to hear that the Berlin Wall had come down. We sank into bed and I slept while Ellen lay awake and worried. The rest is history!'

The rest is history

So, Nuclear Electric had just five months to form itself to be
ready for the flotation of the rest of the electricity supply
industry on 30 March 1990. It had just four years to lick itself
into shape in time for the Nuclear Review. John Collier is a
burly, forthright engineer who was enthusiastic from the first
about communications. He visited the stations regularly and
spoke to the assembled troops. Nuclear Electric inherited from
the CEGB a professional attitude to external and internal
communications. Its newsletter is a model of its kind. Workhouse made video programmes which relayed the Chairman's
goals and, later, explained the new concept of profit and
service centres. Hill & Knowlton was granted a £1.5million PR
contract, reckoned to be the largest awarded during the
recession. J Walter Thompson produced snappy television
commercials and the visitors' centres were refurbished and
equipped with models, visual displays and video walls.

The results were impressive; 260,000 visitors came to the
centres in 1993. A MORI poll revealed that MPs were now
more aware of Nuclear Electric than of the other generators.
Westinghouse approached Nuclear Electric to share in its bid
to build PWRs in Taiwan – an extraordinary compliment to a
company which had not yet completed its own first PWR at
Sizewell. As a bonus, the yacht 'Nuclear Electric', which was
sponsored by the company and skippered by John Chittenden
in the British Steel Challenge, won the 28,000-mile race and
gave the company value-for-money visibility.

Nuclear Electric still faced its biggest communications challenge – the case it would make in its defence during the
government's Nuclear Review in 1994. It was not to be easy.

In the first place, no one could be sure which arm of
government would carry the most power in the Review. If the
Exchequer dominated, the Review was likely, after a deep
recession and in the face of a mounting public sector borrowing
requirement, to take a jaundiced view of the company's need
for capital investment in new PWRs. The Department of the

Environment would take a keen interest in waste disposal and decommissioning. The Department of Trade and Industry would be influenced by the number of high technology jobs created by Nuclear Electric in corners of England and Wales where jobs were scarce, and by the promise of export orders through the Westinghouse alliance. Equally, President of the Board of Trade Michael Heseltine was bound by ideology to recognise the importance of market forces in the electricity supply industry.

Secondly, Nuclear Electric faced difficult decisions as to its best strategy. The biggest questions surrounded the feasibility of privatisation of the company, deeply attractive for the management in that it would remove Nuclear Electric from government interference. Since the Treasury was unlikely to be willing to make public money available for investment in PWRs the company knew it would have to make its case for private investment. Its advisers Price Waterhouse recommended that there was a case for privatisation, but stressed that it would have to be carefully made in light of the City's reluctance just four years before to underwrite nuclear power. In any case, it would be difficult for the company to make public statements about privatisation for fear of offending its sole shareholder, the government.

(Ironically, the case for privatisation carried a sting in its tail. If the company were to go private it would be obliged to follow the laws of the free market. Logic would dictate that it should invest capital not necessarily in nuclear technology but in the assets which would provide the best return for its shareholders, perhaps even the combined cycle gas turbines which were now leading the field. This logic was likely to prove unpopular with the staff of a company whose whole *raison d'etre* had been nuclear technology. This in itself would create a major need for enhanced internal communications.)

Thirdly, the case for nuclear electricity was in itself complex. On the financial front, the company had made outstanding progress in improving the performance particularly of its advanced gas-cooled reactors (AGRs), it now provided a quarter of the electricity consumed in England and Wales and was fast outstripping the second of the fossil-fuelled generators, Powergen. However, critics were quick to point out that the levy represented a large subsidy to Nuclear Electric; it was difficult to explain that the levy had been established purely to compensate for the absence of any funds to meet the liabilities inherited from the CEGB, especially the cost of waste disposal and of decommissioning stations fast approaching the end of their operating lives.

Nuclear Electric had a strong environmental case in that its stations emit virtually no harmful pollutants into the atmosphere. The fossil-fuel stations – particularly with coal – release unacceptable levels of CO_2, (contributing to the greenhouse effect) and the acid rain gases, NOx and SO_2; vast sums would be required to clean up their emissions. However, the nuclear argument was weakened by the absence of underground disposal facilities which meant that radioactive waste produced by nuclear reactors had to be stored above ground, while the by-products of decommissioning would add to the growing pile of hazardous by-products. (Nuclear Electric favours the 'Safe-store' approach to decommissioning – taking the radioactive spent fuel out of the reactor and then wrapping the structure and buildings in a protective shield of stainless steel until the radioactivity has decayed and the building can be dismantled like any other. This method is safer and potentially cheaper but leaves the bulky building on site for up to 100 years.)

Another argument concerned the preservation of high technology skills, many of them in parts of Britain where jobs were not abundant. Nuclear Electric not only employs a large workforce but hires the services of thousands of suppliers, not least when it is building new stations. The construction of Sizewell B had so impressed the American company which designed the PWR – Westinghouse – that Nuclear Electric was invited to join it in a tender for a new reactor to be built in Taiwan. At the time of writing, the result of their joint tender wasn't known but if it is successful, this will provide even more work for Nuclear Electric and its suppliers in Britain.

Safety was also a major concern. John Collier stressed that safety wasn't simply desirable, it was essential to the survival of the business. One serious accident would not only cost untold monies in compensation but would almost certainly result in the closure of all reactors. An important message, but a difficult one to drive home.

Nuclear Electric decided that it needed to explain these issues to an audience of opinion formers whose views might influence the Review itself. It planned to invite national and local politicians, trades union leaders, investment analysts and financial and industrial journalists to small group sessions at which at least one senior member of the company would be present to explain the issues and answer questions. The company approached Workhouse inviting us to prepare proposals for a video programme which would be played at these meetings to set the scene.

The media

It was obvious from the outset that any media would have to be flexible. Policies would change, audiences would differ as would the type and length of session at which the discussions would take place. Sometimes the Chairman, John Collier, or the newly appointed Chief Executive, Dr Bob Hawley, would be present to take part in the debate, more often they would not. The key would lie in the selection not just of one medium, video, but of all relevant media – text, audio, slides – and in using each where it would be most effective.

Nuclear Electric signed on to an approach which, to quote the Head of Public Relations Hugh Price, 'demonstrated the principles of change management in a unique manner. It considered the video as part of a communication strategy which enabled the messages to be communicated by involving the "customer" and without insulting their intelligence.'

Central to the communications package were clear statements of the company's policies by Collier and Hawley, who

were interviewed on video by Michael Blakstad. Both are
articulate and forceful communicators; in preparing for the
interview they had taken care to harmonise their message and
simplify its delivery. These were powerful performances which
were intercut throughout the video modules. Even when one
of the two was present at the screenings, he allowed the pre-
recorded video sequences to do this part of the talking since
these represented the most succinct and clear statements of the
case.

This clarity was achieved in part through the close liaison
which took place between the production company and the
senior management. It was obvious from the outset that the
company would have to dedicate considerable internal
resources to the project. As Hugh Price said, 'although
Workhouse would produce the material, we would be the
owners'. A project manager was appointed; Dr Julie Corbett is
a young engineer recently appointed as technical assistant to
the Executive Directors, with direct access to the Chairman
and Chief Executive and with first-hand knowledge of the
issues with which we were dealing. This was to be her first
project in the new post, and she now picks up the story in her
own words:

> Workhouse had recommended, and we were fully signed
> on to the following principles:
>
> * Communication is a two-way process; it is more effec-
>   tive to stimulate debate about an issue than to present
>   an audience or individual with a closed case.
> * People only have a limited time span of attention, so a
>   varied interactive presentation will be much more
>   effective than a long monologue.
> * People are accustomed to receiving information through a
>   variety of media – television or video, audio, written ma-
>   terial, discussion, hands-on experience. School teachers
>   have been working successfully on this principle for
>   years.
> * Messages are retained better if they are reinforced on
>   one or more occasions after the initial communication.

There couldn't be a clearer statement of the principles of the use of media in corporate communication. Even though the primary audience for this package was to be people outside the company, it was necessary to win their support not for a single moment or for a straightforward message. They were to be made advocates in the same way as internal staff are to be persuaded to 'own' a company strategy or culture. Julie Corbett continues:

> Based on these basic principles of communication, and a detailed briefing on Nuclear Electric's background, present performance and strategy going into the Review, Workhouse produced a package consisting of the following:

> - An *audio tape* produced in the style of a Radio 4 documentary. This is about 15 minutes long and can be listened to in the car, at home or in the office. It reviews the background to the company and the arguments for and against nuclear power in a colourful and provocative way. It is aimed at reminding the listener of the issues and ensuring that they arrive at the presentation interested and ready to talk.
> - a *video programme* which consists of four short modules, each addressing one of the main areas for focus in the Review. Although the terms of reference of the Review were not known at the time of planning we felt it appropriate to cover each of the main areas due to their strategic inter-relatedness. These can be given the appropriate weighting for the audience in question. Each module of the video is played in turn, and each followed by a discussion which can be as long or short as time allows.
> - a *booklet* containing some of the detailed facts and figures and detailed arguments behind the issues. Experience has shown that over half the questions arising from the viewing of the video can be answered by reference to the booklet. Care should be taken to make absolutely sure that the key messages are both clear and accessible.

- the *presenter*. The tools in the communications package do not replace the presenter, but rather support
her or him. They free the hands and mind from the
slides – our traditional audio-visual aid – and enable
the presenter to react more freely with the audience.

In a programme as detailed as this, relating to an industry
as complex as ours and with a public perception challenge
as taxing as the one facing us, the content and tone had to
be just right. To some extent these are mutually contradic-
tory requirements. My task was to have all of the relevant
experts and wielders of corporate authority check,
approve and sign on to the content proposed by Workhouse. This involved considerable effort. Workhouse had
to ensure that the product ended up with the style and
tone that would make the argument accessible to the
intended audience.

The 32-page booklet was based on the theory that busy people
will typically spend only four minutes scanning an unsolicited
document. It was desktop published in such a way that the
unmotivated reader could quickly read a number of bullet
points or headlines which highlight the argument – 'It is fast
becoming a financially viable business' . . . 'over 100,000
British jobs depend on the nuclear industry' . . . 'The UK is
committed to returning its CO_2 emissions to their 1990 level by
the year 2000' and so on. An example of the lively typographical
style is illustrated:

THE *avoidable cost* OF
Magnox generation
IS *1.3p/kWh*

We hoped that these headlines would intrigue readers sufficiently to persuade them to read the 'mainstream' of the argument which runs like a typographical river through the booklet. Its islands and headlands are a series of boxes and diagrams in which some of the more complex arguments and technical terms are briefly explained. The printed booklet was to be the permanent reminder and reference point once the seminar was over, to reinforce what had been said and provide some answers to lingering questions.

Before the media had been finalised, they were extensively piloted in draft and rough-cut form, as Dr Corbett describes:

> The final approval was to be given by the Board of Directors, not least because these would be the most important users of the material. Prior to presentation to the Board, it was tested on several internal audiences. This internal approval process and the many briefing sessions for users that were to follow Board approval, turned out to be a more significant step in the process than we had expected. This was because it was for many of the Directors, Heads of Functions, Managers and Talks Service Speakers the first time they had been brought together to discuss the company's policies and strategy and how best to present these to the world. Not only were they being taught how the tool worked, but were contributing to the development of the tool. In this way the very principles on which the package was based were being used to market it!
>
> As you'd expect, individual members of staff differed in their reactions – from each other, or from the corporate approach. In some instances people were simply not adequately informed or hadn't talked through the issues with others of a differing viewpoint. More often the process of debating the issues resulted in a sharing of approaches from which everybody benefited.

Enrol your owners

The tool-kit had two main purposes. The first was to ensure that staff within Nuclear Electric understood all the key issues in the development of the company towards privatisation. The second was that they could then use this knowledge and elements of the tool-kit to influence specific groups of decision makers and also to inform the public as a whole.

The use of the media to enlist the support of Nuclear Electric's own staff for the company's message before it was communicated to outside audiences was successful and confirmed Workhouse's belief in the benefits that companies gain through staff involvement in this type of process. As we have seen, they are its best ambassadors.

They were fortunate that there was time to adopt this approach. The company had originally been led to expect that the terms of reference would be published in September 1993; Michael Heseltine's heart attack and ministerial in-fighting delayed the process by fully nine months. The 'media tool-kit' was ready in the autumn of 1993. This gave the company a breathing space in which the internal briefings took place.

However, Hugh Price feels that the external campaign has not been wholly successful. The tool-kit has not been used as extensively as was planned at the Pall Mall headquarters of Nuclear Electric to which national opinion formers were to be invited in order to view and discuss it, partly because of government delays which have made it harder for the board to agree tactics.

On the other hand, the Nuclear Review programme has been used extensively and to considerable effect in local communities around the country. Julie Corbett has since been promoted to an operating unit at Wylfa in North Wales where she reports that the programme has been regularly and success-fully used with local politicians and civic dignitaries. She relates how the process of testing the product and coaching the intended facilitators meant that the pack came to be used for:

> a much wider range of audiences than had ever been in-tended by Nuclear Electric, including schools and societies. In addition, we assessed its potential for internal communi-

cations. We were well aware that our staff, in their homes,
leisure pursuits and involvement with their local communities are among our most important influencers. The
main task here was to convince managers that it is a
worthwhile investment of staff time rather than a cosmetic
exercise.

At the end of the day, the Nuclear Review programme, as the
media tool-kit was known, may well have had more effect on
its internal audiences than on the external opinion formers for
whom it had originally been commissioned. Hugh Price reports
that it produced a 'coherence in the company about what our
policy is . . .' – which he admits was an unexpected by-product
of a public relations exercise. 'The company now knows what
the policy is, down to the most lowly operative.' It is for this
reason that we have included this case study alongside the
other employee communications projects reported in this
book.

In September 1994 *The Money Programme* devoted half an
edition to the nuclear debate. The reporter Richard Watson
was succinct in his analysis of Nuclear Electric and its privatisation campaign. Despite the appearance in the programme of
well-known environmentalists like Jonathan Porritt, his arguments were overwhelmingly in favour of the company. They
echoed in some detail the content and logic of the Nuclear
Review programme – yet he had never been exposed directly to
the media tool-kit. Perhaps Hugh Price was right and the
representatives of Nuclear Electric had fully absorbed the company's case and briefed Watson accordingly. At the end of the
day, any company's best ambassadors will always be its people –
and if Nuclear Electric does win out in the end, it is them it
should thank.

The nuclear message could not have been carried as effectively
on a single medium. Audio set out the context of the debate and
saved time at presentations. The short video triggers by the
articulate leadership of the company guaranteed a clear consistent message. The bullet points at the end of the modules, and
the ensuing debate from them, helped to fix the essential points

in the audiences minds and the text allowed the simple expression of complex arguments and statistics.

The situation in our next case, Railtrack, was very different. This was an organisation in change. Its internal audience was spread in small groups with enormous geographical dispersion often working at locations with no obvious facilities for any complex communications. The organisation was facing considerable reorganisation as a preparation for privatisation. This was creating a major internal dispute with major external implications. The communications message was complex and there had to be rapid settlement.

Railtrack – Pulling the Communication Cord

Railtrack recently faced a more urgent communications need than that experienced by any of our other case study companies. In addition, its communications were being played out in a very public arena in the middle of a national dispute which was affecting every aspect of life in the UK.

Major change in any organisation poses a communication challenge to managers. Communicating change in an organisation where the managers themselves are new, and where access to staff can only begin once the change has taken place, poses a double challenge. Operating under these circumstances and in the face of a mounting industrial dispute creates the toughest of communications challenges.

In April 1994 the British railway industry was totally restructured, breaking the monolithic British Rail (BR) down into dozens of component businesses, with responsibility for the rolling stock, running services, maintenance and the infrastructure. Railtrack – the largest of the new businesses – was created to own and manage the 11,000-mile network, its stations, signals and bridges. An organisation of 12,000 people was created virtually overnight.

Those Railtrack managers who worked on the preparations for the new company wanted to begin to put a communications structure in place before the restructuring date of 1 April. But they couldn't do so before the official date for the break-up of BR. And their ambitions for communications were thwarted by the industrial storm clouds that were already looming by that time.

For years the signal workers who formed the core of Railtrack's employees had been arguing with BR over productivity payments for the rationalisation of signal boxes all over the country. The issue had been passed from year to year, and the simmering resentment had grown into genuine anger. Within weeks of arriving at Railtrack, they voted for industrial action.

Railtrack had resisted the pressure to pay more for past productivity gains, but wanted to introduce a total restructuring of signalling pay and conditions to replace the archaic structure that had existed under BR. That structure gave staff very low levels of basic pay, supplemented by a plethora of allowances, some of which dated back half a century. Railtrack proposed replacing this with a higher basic pay rate, fewer allowances, and some extra money for the introduction of a more flexible working environment. The management believed that the new offer was positive for the vast majority of employees but recognised that understanding this required a very complex set of arguments. Traditionally, workers in the railway industry have relied on their unions to explain any offers. The union rejected the proposal and the battle lines were drawn.

The Communications Group of senior managers which had begun mapping out plans for communication found itself handling crisis communications rather than building long-term bridges across the organisation. The group was also faced with the challenge of reaching individuals in remote locations, often far from their home bases and with no access to or experience of any sophisticated communications media.

Throughout the dispute the company focused its attention on providing as much information as possible directly to staff, to counter the communications channels that already existed within the signal union, the National Union of Rail, Maritime and Transport Workers (RMT).

Communication responsibilities were divided between the company's London head office and the individual geographic zones into which Railtrack's organisation was divided. From the centre, Railtrack sent out to staff a series of regular bulletins explaining the company's position and its perspective of developments during the dispute. Senior directors, including the Chairman, Robert Horton, also visited a number of operational sites to talk to striking staff (see Chapter 5).

In the zones, senior managers were able to use the existing team-briefing structure that they had inherited from British Rail to keep a flow of information group – though the structure was more effective in some areas than others. The Zone Directors also visited as many signal boxes as possible on days when the men were at work to argue the company's position. A special computer programme was made available to managers to explain to individuals how they personally would be affected by the change.

The zones opened hot lines which gave staff a chance to give their reaction to the proposals and to indicate where anxieties remained. This helped the core team who had been working on the proposals to recast the package into a form that would finally settle the dispute.

The media

After nearly three months of one- and two-day strikes, the combination of the financial pressure on staff, the success of managers in keeping key parts of the network open, and the communications effort paid off. A conference of signalling staff mandated union negotiators to meet the company at ACAS, and a settlement was quickly reached.

It was clear that simple communication from the Railtrack management would be needed as soon as agreement was reached to cut through the media obfuscation that had confused so many of the signal workers. In the latter stages of the dispute, Railtrack worked hard to ensure that it grasped the communication initiative at the end of the negotiations process – and prepared a series of briefing documents for staff and managers to explain the settlement when it was reached. It looked carefully at video and audio options but eventually rejected these on the grounds of speed of production, difficulty of rapid distribution and the problem of access to replay facilities. Text was clearly the medium which was not only comfortable and familiar to the highly technical audience of signal workers but which was also one that could be produced rapidly and distributed within hours to remote signal boxes or directly to homes without relying on any presentation technology.

Text frameworks were developed which could be adapted to accommodate the final details of the agreed settlement. These frameworks were constructed of simple illustrations and clear summary bullet points so that the information could be absorbed rapidly within a high pressure working environment and which could then be studied in detail at a later time.

While the final two days of talks took place at ACAS, the discussions were shadowed by the communications team at Railtrack, preparing the material to go to print as soon as agreement was reached. When the union indicated that it would accept, at 11pm on the Tuesday night, the first publication, an eight-page booklet explaining the agreed terms, was delivered to the printer. When the deal was ratified five hours later, the presses rolled.

The printed booklet was available for the company's press conference at 10.30 that morning, and was in all 10 zones for distribution to staff that afternoon. A second, more substantial booklet giving managers full details of the package to enable them to answer questions from staff was distributed by fax the same day, and in printed form shortly afterwards.

The response from both managers and signalling staff was highly positive, and Railtrack executives believed that the rapid move to distribute detailed information to all involved cast the company in a very favourable light at a time when it needed to begin building bridges.

The lesson of the importance of communication has not been lost within the company. With the subsequent announcement of privatisation has come a clear determination on the part of senior managers to inform and involve staff about what is going on, to make sure that communication is a two-way process, to listen to the views of staff and to act decisively. It's a lesson that no organisation can afford to ignore.

Simple guidelines

A look at the two case studies in this chapter and the variety of cases discussed elsewhere in this book illustrates the difficulties that communications managers face in selecting the best media mix to carry their messages. Let us look at a simple set of five different media options:

- Personal presentation
- Text
- Audio
- Video
- Electronic media.

In addition, at the beginning of the chapter we indicated that there are six main factors which affect media selection:

- Message
- Audience
- Time
- Environment
- Ability
- Cost.

Life would be very simple if these could be simply plotted against each other to provide an easy answer, as in the following table:

Factors	Personal presentation	Text	Audio	Video	Electronic media
Message					
Audience					
Time					
Environment					
Ability					
Cost					

The real difficulty is that the possible permutations from combinations of the factors in column 1 are almost infinite. It is a truly multidimensional problem. This means that it is almost impossible to define a single, simple set of rules that will guarantee the selection of the perfect vehicles for delivering effective communications. However, there are some guidelines which can help. In the following pages we have tried to indicate where different media are likely to be of most effect and where they are likely to be positively dangerous. It may seem like applied common sense, but it is quite extraordinary how even the simplest lessons are frequently forgotten.

Personal presentation

Message   Provided that it is supported by other appropriate media, personal presentation is a highly effective way of carrying out most internal corporate communications. Communications should be a two-way process and a well-trained facilitator is able to interact with the audience and to answer any questions that may be raised, to parry counter-arguments or to carry back reactions, moods, suggestions and ideas.

However, there must be considerable care in selecting the individuals or team who are to act as presenters/

facilitators and to ensure that they are well briefed themselves and that they have the presentation skills necessary to carry out the task. The presenters must also have credibility with respect to the particular message that they are communicating. Also, no matter how well a presentation may be scripted or supported by other media, presenters can add their own interpretations very easily. It may not be the words that they say, or don't say. It may just be the body language that they use or the looks on their faces which alter the message.

Organisations often opt for cascade communications without bothering to ensure that their presenters are credible or competent. This not only serves to reduce the effectiveness of the immediate communication but also reduces the credibility of future efforts.

Audience   Different groups within organisations often develop and use their own jargon and style of presentation. A message which will be clear to a group of senior executives is not necessarily credible or intelligible to administrative staff or to those in development, production, marketing or customer service. The selection of presenters and facilitators needs to be guided carefully by the expectations and common cultures of the audience. However, there are some messages that need the full authority or charisma of the chairman or chief executive.

The size and geographical distribution of the audience is an obvious issue which will affect whether personal presentation is a possibility and who can be selected to carry it out. If an audience is small and at a single location, personal presentation is nearly always the best and most cost-effective option. As size and geographical distribution of the audience grow, the control of the consistency of the message reduces in inverse proportion and the logistics of organising the presentations increases.

Time   If time is absolutely of the essence, it is often quicker and simpler to use personal presentations than any other option. However, control and consistency may be lost.

Environment   Unless the message is clear and simple, the environment can be a key factor in guaranteeing understanding and acceptance of personally presented communications. Audiences need to be comfortable in the environment where they are receiving a message. There should be relatively little interference from other stimuli. This doesn't mean that the location must be quiet or even calm. Research shows that people's attention is often raised by the presence of familiar sounds.

Ability   Most people are bad communicators and don't realise it. They are ill-trained at organising a message, bad at using media support and appalling at listening. Successful organisations ensure intensive training programmes for their communicators.

Cost   The cost of personal presentation is often lower than other options. However, although cost may seem low it is important to look at the cost of training presenters, the opportunity cost of losing them from other activities and the travel and subsistence costs of getting speakers to the right locations. Sometimes the cost is a great deal higher than it appears at first.

Text

Message   Text is very powerful at both presenting clear summaries of information and in allowing the presentation of high levels of complex detail or explanation which may need concerted study. The message does not need to be in words alone but can be effectively enhanced with graphics, diagrams and pictures to create the required level of redundancy and reinforcement to ensure capture of the information. It should be remembered that one of the most effective uses of text is ensuring that there is plenty of clear space around the message and in providing space for receivers to note down comments.

Text can also play a positive role in stimulating feedback to facilitate the two-way flow of information. Well-designed questionnaires, response forms or action plans can play a vital role in this process.

Audience   Text is a familiar medium for all corporate audiences. However, communications managers do need to bear in mind that the type of text that is comfortable and intelligible to one group in the organisation may be

disconcerting and opaque to another. There is a terrible
tendency to adopt the highest common denominator
approach to the preparation of all media in corporate
communications rather than analysing the expectations
and abilities of the audience.

Text is a very effective way of reaching large and far-
flung audiences quickly with a consistent structured message.

Time Today, the advances in electronic publishing
have meant that well-designed text can be produced
quickly and efficiently. However, the ease with which text
can now be produced has led many managers to believe
that they are design experts. This has led to the creation of
appalling packages of materials which confuse rather than
clarify the message. Taking a little extra time to test
materials, or using a design expert in the first place can
pay dividends.

Environment Text is a familiar, comfortable medium
which is usually completely portable. It can come in a
wide variety of forms from posters to news sheets, books
to prompt cards. It can be used in almost any location
either as a stand-alone item or as a support to presentations or other media.

However, care should be taken about some aspects of
text. For instance, some companies have created posters
which have been put up in locations or have been in
formats which are easily altered or defaced. This can
change the message radically, make it humorous and
destroy the intended impact.

Ability Ability of presenters does not tend to be a real
issue with text except in terms of the way in which it is
introduced. Ability to design effective text is far more
specialised than is usually realised.

Cost Print costs can vary enormously. Excellent print
design can be costly and top quality colour reproduction
can be very expensive. However, this can sometimes be
counter-productive. Excessively over-engineered print
can produce resentment in audiences who are being
restricted on pay and other budgets or who would normally expect simpler production. With good design, text
can be produced to low budgets and can be reproduced
and packaged at very reasonable cost.

Audio

Message   Audio is a very 'affective' medium. It forces
people to use their imaginations and to set information
and messages into the context of their own experience. It
is more emotional than rational. In addition it is a
powerful and cost-effective way of allowing people to
listen to the views of others within their own organisation
and to sample a variety of opinions. Because of its ease of
use audiences can be encouraged to play audio material a
number of times to ensure that they have absorbed a
message fully or to look at it from a variety of different
perspectives.

Most people are used to listening to radio news and it
seems that this gives audio a high level of credibility.

It is not a good medium for transmitting detailed factual
or numerical information.

Audience   Most audiences respond well to the use of
audio communications. There will be few people who do
not have access to the equipment to replay audio either
through personal hi-fis, through tape players in their cars
or more sophisticated equipment at home or in the office.

It is an excellent way to reach almost all audiences,
large and small. Translation and re-recording into other
languages for international use is frequently cost-
effective.

The one note of caution is once again to ensure that the
language used is palatable to the audience.

Time   Audio programmes can be made relatively
quickly. Modern editing equipment gives considerable
flexibility in production. After text it is probably the
quickest option to adopt.

Environment   Modern audio equipment allows cas-
settes to be played in an almost infinite variety of surroundings with ease.

Ability   Few people would find the use of audio equipment difficult.

Cost   Cost is low. It is possible to produce audio
programmes for less than a quarter of the cost of the
average video programme of the same length and style.

However, depending on the nature of the message, it may
have less effect.

Video

Message   Video is very powerful when used correctly.
Properly designed it allows the compression of a message
into a much shorter time than any other medium. It is best
suited to simple summary statements made by key
communicators within an organisation who cannot be
present personally with all the intended audiences. Video
is good at presenting short, sharp messages illustrated
with clear graphics and reinforced through the use of the
right tempo of music and complementary captions. It is
not good for transmitting substantial quantities of facts,
numerical information or complex arguments.

Information that is presented on video is retained by the
audience to a far higher degree than the same information
provided through other media.

It is an exciting medium which can engage the audience
and prepare them for action or encourage them to become
involved in a process. Messages on video are usually
presented best by people within the organisation or from a
related company. Media stars and professional presenters
tend to increase costs and reduce credibility.

Audience   Most of today's audiences are sophisticated
television viewers. It is important to recognise that their
expectations of on-screen presentation may not be the
same as the management who are designing a programme.
It is no use making a video look like *Panorama* if most of
the audience watch *The Big Breakfast*. Too often
managers make videos of themselves in situations that
represent their fantasies rather than choosing a style to
engage the audience and enhance communication.

In addition to being a powerful aid to personal presentation or to acting as the focus of facilitated sessions, video
is most frequently of use with a large dispersed audience.

Time   Good video takes time to produce. It needs
careful design, checking and production to have most
impact. It can however be completed rapidly to communi-

cate essential urgent messages by the development of frameworks which are adapted to the specific details of the message, such as end of year results.

Environment   Today the majority of individuals have access to video cassette players at home. The difficulty is in motivating audiences to actually play the videos. Research has shown that many corporate videos are watched by less than 10 per cent of the intended audience.

Replay of video in large presentations or away from a home base can cause problems. The impact of good video can be destroyed easily by poor presentation facilities. The problems can range from badly maintained equipment, through inadequate screens or sound systems for the size of audience, through to poor lighting conditions which reduce the visibility of the screen. This is particularly true when video projector systems are used.

The assumption that people will watch videos at home is also often wrong. The demands on the use of the average home television set are often high. Research has shown that there are strong levels of resentment to being forced to watch a company video at home. However, the right type of presentation can be motivating and the home environment can involve partners and other family members in a commitment to a corporate message.

Ability   Although nearly everybody has a video recorder at home, using video as part of a presentation requires more skill than many managers believe. In unfamiliar surroundings setting up the video player and making sure that the TV is tuned to the right channel, sound levels are correct etc can prove problematic. Effective use of video needs careful rehearsal and, except in exceptionally well-equipped presentation rooms, it is often helpful for someone other than the speaker to manage the equipment.

Cost   Despite the reduction in the prices of sophisticated video production equipment, the cost of producing effective video programmes is still often quite high. While incorporating 'home made – self-shot' video into programmes can prove to be very effective, the final product still requires the skills of highly professional staff to structure messages effectively and to set them within a quality framework. None the less, it is probably true that the average 'cost per minute' of video production has stayed constant in numerical terms across the last 20 years which represents a considerable reduction in real terms.

Electronic media

Message   Electronic media can be used to carry almost any type of message from the simplest memo to the illustration of complex arguments. The power of computing within an electronic system can allow dynamic presentation of numerical arguments through animated graphics or through providing opportunities for the receiver to manipulate numbers and test propositions.

It is also possible to accompany a simple summary message with a complete set of supportive information for access by those receivers who want to review further data.

Audience   Very few audiences are comfortable yet with electronic media. Studies have shown that the installation of sophisticated internal electronic communications networks does not necessarily improve the circulation of information nor contribute to strengthening corporate culture. However, those companies that have made conscious efforts to incorporate electronic media into their standard business processes appear to have gained substantial performance improvements.

Communications options via traditional telecoms, cable and satellite are developing rapidly. The improvement in bandwidths on these systems will provide increasing capacity for electronic communications ranging from simple voice and text through to sophisticated on-demand video distribution and desktop television.

The development of the domestic entertainment market is another factor which will improve audience ability and acceptance. Market trends in the USA indicate a rapid expansion of acquisition of sophisticated multimedia equipment in the home. The French experience of the take up and use of Minitel also provides indicators of a positive future for this technology. Trends in the UK parallel the US picture with a lag at present of about two years. There is an accelerating trend for electronic media in the home and the office. A recent study has shown that by 1999 sophisticated computing and communications systems will be commonplace in the majority of UK homes and offices.

Time   The time-scale for the development and distribution of communications via electronic media varies enormously. Simple electronic mail can be sent almost instantly, direct to the desk of the intended recipient anywhere in the world. The development of sophisticated interactive products can be very time-consuming. Each communication needs a fresh review.

Environment   The options are almost unlimited. Electronic media can be used to support personal presentation by providing instant access to a database of images, facts or video to allow considerable flexibility of response. At present few organisations are set up to manage this type of presentation. Eventually, electronic media will be able to give secure access to communications to any individual in almost any location which has access to a telephone line or other communications link.

Ability   Even the simplest electronic communications require a higher level of ability than currently possessed by most people in UK industry, commerce and public sector organisations. There is a considerable training job to be carried out. However, it is expected that in a relatively short period the skills of using more sophisticated electronic media will become as much a part of the fabric of office life as using the telephone is today.

A high level of varied skills are needed at present to develop complex interactive communications. For this reason, very few organisations are likely to maintain dedicated teams 'in-house'. However, more advanced 'authoring tools' are being produced which can link with existing databases and communications technology inside organisations and which offer more flexible options for the future.

Cost   Although the price of information technology is still falling rapidly, the true cost is still high. The actual annual unit cost of installing and maintaining a computer-based workstation is between six and 20 times the purchase price. There are also further costs in time lost and wasted through inefficient or unnecessary use. However, these costs should be set against some of the savings that can be made in travel, subsistence and other areas. In the longer term, efficiency improvements and continually falling costs will make electronic media an attractive option.

In this chapter we have looked at two cases with very different needs and have reviewed how they chose the media to communicate their messages. We have also reviewed a number of factors for the most common media in use today or likely to be introduced in the near future. The main points to learn are set out below.

Checklist

1. *Analyse* each situation carefully. In particular make sure that the audience is clearly understood in terms of its expectations, culture, numbers, location and dispersion. The definition of the audience is often the primary factor in selecting media. The nature of the message and the desired outcome is the second most important issue.
2. *Train* the presenters or facilitators in using the media selected and make sure that they are both technically competent and that they understand all the nuances of each communications campaign.
3. *Cost* out each campaign realistically and place a value on achieving the objectives. Use these figures to guide the selection of media. The true costs are sometimes substantially higher than appears at first sight. Using senior executives for personal presentations can sometimes be prohibitively expensive when set against the opportunity cost of their time. Likewise, try to place a real value on achieving the objectives. This too can often be substantially higher than a simple analysis might indicate. A marginal improvement in employee job satisfaction or the reduction of uncertainty can have a major effect on the bottom line.

7

■ We Have the Technology – BT and IBM

This chapter differs from the others in that it does not tell the story of change programmes but surveys the technologies available to the communicating organisation. The two companies concerned, BT and IBM, have both undertaken massive downsizing programmes and both are in the public eye, which means they have to move rapidly to brief their staff more quickly than the media can carry the news. But their place in this book is due to the fact that they both make and market the technologies of communication – telephony and computers.

It is a consequence of downsizing and outsourcing – two of the buzz-words of the 1990s – that communication is becoming harder than ever. Many of the people laid off by their employers end up working as consultants or suppliers for the same companies, on short-term contracts and from their own premises, often their homes. These outworkers are part of the new corporate family and are subject to the same laws of motivation and loyalty as their erstwhile colleagues working inside company buildings. They don't want to be fed one-way, one-off messages and they haven't the same access to the office grapevine.

In many respects, these outworkers present the same challenge as the traditional army of salespeople, signalmen, repair engineers, patrolmen and drivers whose work keeps them on the road for most of their working lives and for whom it is difficult to organise any coherent pattern of meetings.

BT's workforce operate in offices spread around towns and cities throughout Britain, or in grey vans, or up poles and down holes. During the past decade BT has shed tens of thousands of staff, following privatisation and growing competition from Mercury, Racal, Energis and other companies which are now challenging it for a slice of Britain's profitable telecommunications market. However, BT does have one enormous advantage in communicating with its workforce – it has the technology.

So does IBM. Like BT, Big Blue has been forced in recent years to reduce considerably its levels of staff; faced with unprecedented financial losses in the early 1990s, the mighty organisation has been obliged radically to redesign its structure. Not only have many thousands of people been laid off but those who stayed have been reorganised into self-contained units with clear business objectives. Many such units have now been sold, often to their own staff.

The county of Hampshire, in which the majority of IBM activities in Britain were based, has witnessed the birth of dozens of niche consultancies and agencies formed by executives who have left IBM and set up on their own account. In short, the company has needed to introduce change on a scale and at a speed unmatched even by the other companies reported in this book.

However, this chapter does not attempt to report how the two giants managed their change programmes. Instead, we focus on the technologies which BT and IBM have developed to sell to customers – but which each has used in facing up to its own need to communicate with its staff.

Dynamic duo

BT's medium is telecommunications, the transmission of messages across distances great and small. IBM's is computing, the control of digital signals so that data can be harnessed and processed. The combination of telecommunications and computing opens a Pandora's box of media which place unprecedented power at the elbow of the corporate communicator and, as we shall see, the fun has only just begun.

IBM and BT are so large that their activities attract constant media attention. Both are so geographically diverse that it is often hard for the companies themselves to communicate with their staff before television, radio or the newspapers have relayed their version of latest developments straight into the sitting-rooms of every member of staff.

Mike Bett, President of the IPD, has also been Chief Executive and deputy chairman of BT. Bett has always believed that the pre-eminent means of communicating with staff is the human being, 'Videos can't listen,' he says. The same goes for BT's Controller of Employee Communications, Brenda McAll; they both believe strongly in personal contact as the leading edge of employee communications – when it can be achieved.

Face to face

Brenda McAll spearheads the communication of management messages to BT people and the collection of feedback. 'Face to face is key to employee communications,' says Brenda, 'Team meetings and walking the job are still the best means.' She is, for instance, responsible for the roadshows which today's Group Managing Director, Michael Hepher, regularly stages for employees. Management roadshows take place annually, visiting eight cities around Britain and bringing Michael Hepher directly into contact with the company's senior and middle managers – 6,500 of them in all. These roadshows 'kick off' the year, setting the agenda for new initiatives and developments; Brenda McAll points out: 'debate is the most important part. We limit the "dump" – the formal presentation – to 20 minutes. The two meetings in London, with 2,000 managers gathered in to Wembley Conference Centre, use roving microphones to encourage audience participation but tend to be a bit unwieldy.'

Face to face also dictates the monthly meetings in which every member of BT is involved; these allow discussions to take place at a local level. The challenge comes in spreading urgent messages through such a large organisation spread across every corner of Britain. 'We can't arrange face-to-face

meetings at short notice with the man who garages his van at
home and phones in for his assignments.'

This is where the technology of telecommunications comes
into play. BT's armoury of media includes business television,
teletext, fax, electronic mail, information retrieval systems,
recorded news services . . . and more besides.

Newsline

Newsline deploys the technology of the telephone answering
service, on the grand scale. It is a 24-hour-a-day, seven-days-a-
week, dial-up news service for employees available on an 0800
number. Being free, people can call from home if they wish. It
can be updated in minutes, several times a week, or even
several times a day. BT had a quarter of a million calls in its
first year and the take-up is still rising – BT recorded its
millionth phone call in the autumn of 1994.

One of the great benefits of this particular channel is that it
enables managers to graft facts directly onto the grapevine
which, of course, remains one of the most influential communications media. Each of those callers will talk to colleagues and
customers – and Newsline helps bring more consistency and
control to such informal contacts. Nor does it matter whether
any employee is office-based or not – all he or she needs is
access to a phone, any time of day or night.

The fax

Another of its own products which BT uses to the full extent
for its own people is the fax. (I almost wrote, 'traditional' – it is
surprising how far the fax has penetrated into our lives in a
relatively short time.) All the BT services described in this
chapter can be linked to a fax information retrieval system
(FIRS) and those who need further information can request a
hard copy. 'For example,' says McAll, 'when communicating
financial results, the headline figures can be given on Newsline

and teletext and anyone who wants more detail can call off hard copy by fax. FIRS is also used in conjunction with BT's employee briefings which can now be supported by a telephone number to ring for hard copy of further information. Everyone gets the big message; the detail goes only to those who want it.'

She continues, 'The great beauty of fax information retrieval is that it is energy efficient. You only get the paper to the people who need and want it, thereby saving trees and avoiding information overload. Communication of this kind is customer- rather than supplier-driven, and that is a key change.' Another example, given the spread of fax machines into homes, is that this form of communication can reach the field operators as well as the officers. Many service engineers now carry portable message terminals which can keep them in touch wherever they are.

Electronic mail

Where BT's business is telecommunications, IBM's is computing; when the two technologies are linked, their power to communicate is virtually unconfined. The majority of desks in business today carry some form of workstation, and many of these are connected to a network which enables the computers to relay information from one to another. Most such networks are contained within one building or site (Local Area Networks – LANs); some connect sites across a wide geographic spread (Wide Area Networks – WANs).

For 20 years now, companies have been using electronic mail (e-mail) as a means of sending text messages along lines and onto screens as an alternative to paperwork sent through the internal mail and into the in-tray. To take just one example, the bureau F International, which creates jobs for women working at home, uses e-mail as a fast and inexpensive means of communicating with its army of 'outworkers'.

The Industrial Society survey reported in Chapter 2 indicated that communications managers have misgivings about e-mail; it is regarded as an unfriendly medium – a text message blinking on a screen seems to some to be the nadir of remote control, a take-it-or-leave-it signal like so many impersonal messages on company noticeboards. It may take a generation before computers can lay claim to the description which they introduced to the jargon dictionary: 'user-friendly'.

Companies which use e-mail need, therefore, to consider its weaknesses as well as its strengths before allowing it to replace completely the telephone call or face-to-face encounters as the main means of communicating with their people. One of its strengths is the speed with which a message can reach large numbers of offices, a facility of which IBM makes full use.

Beating the media

The computer giant shares with BT yet another challenge; it too is a large and widespread company and has attracted a great deal of media attention, particularly during the early 1990s when the company went through its most agonising period of staff reduction. Paul Weston, until recently the communications manager at IBM's North Harbour centre near Portsmouth, describes the inadequacy of paper communications which used to take two days to reach most people – 'by which time the news had appeared in yesterday's newspaper.' IBM operates an e-mail news service entitled 'Today'; it is regularly crammed with information about the company – to the point where some staff may find that they can't read every bulletin every time it is changed.

To make sure that its people don't miss the important messages, 'Today' will carry a message announcing that 'results will be posted at 3pm today' – for example – to create an awareness among managers that they have a task to perform in that they must read the news when it appears and ensure that their teams are also updated before they read, hear or see the coverage in their news media.

IBM works hard to ensure that the process is two-way. For

instance, it has established a readers' panel to measure attitudes to the company newspaper. After each issue the editor
sends a series of questions down the e-mail system to the panel
asking for reactions, 'understood?', 'need more information?'
and so forth. The editor encourages IBM people to debate the
issues and send reactions down the line or to contact him for
further information. Weston reports that attitudes to the
newspaper have improved considerably since e-mail was used
in this way to create feedback.

Speak-up!

If e-mail is the workhorse of internal communications via
computer, IBM is using its network for other means which aid
the upward flow of employees' issues and concerns. One
example is its 'Speak-up!' system, which allows employees the
chance to conduct a debate with their bosses without having to
reveal their identities.

In open meetings, people are often inhibited from expressing their true opinions for fear either of their bosses or simply
of expressing a minority opinion. People with dominant personalities all too often inhibit the expression of alternative views
from more timid but not necessarily less imaginative people.
Using the on-line Speak-up! system, people enter their views
directly onto their own workstations, whence it is fed onto the
screen of a co-ordinator. Only the co-ordinator knows the
identity of the originator. The text is then encrypted and
forwarded on to the appropriate executive director for reply.

It is the electronic version of the complaints or suggestions
box. Anyone in the company can enter a complaint or
suggestion onto his or her workstation in the absolute knowledge that the bosses will never know the source of the signal. If
anyone in IBM, however senior, asks the co-ordinator who is
responsible for expressing a specific view on the Speak-up!
system, this is a breach of discipline which could warrant
dismissal from the company.

Business Television Network

BT produces a regular, fortnightly, live news programme for managers. The programme is encrypted, to safeguard confidential material, then broadcast over a satellite link and decoded before it is shown in over 400 offices and viewing areas across the country, such as staff restaurants, conference rooms and lobbies.

BT sometimes has to release price-sensitive information. Legally, such news must be issued to the Stock Exchange before it is communicated to the management of BT. The danger here lies in staff hearing it through the broadcast media before the internal channels are able to deliver it. 'Now,' says McAll, 'within half an hour of releasing the news to the Stock Exchange at 7.30am, BT's managers are able to see the top team talking live about the results – and analysts commenting on them – whilst everyone else in the company can get the essential information from Newsline.'

The one-off investment in business television is large; BT keeps the cost of programme-making down by operating its own modest studios. Satellite costs will come down as more companies use the service. The principal obstacle to business television lies, according to McAll, in the high cost of producing programmes. She believes the video production sector is slowing down the growth of business television by demanding unrealistically high prices for making the programme. 'We make our programmes in-house – we already had a studio and editing equipment. We make the programmes for around £3,000 each which makes economic sense when they are seen by such a large audience. It makes less sense when production companies quote prices of over £20,000. Their argument is that viewers are used to the production values of primetime television with lots of location filming and professional presenters. It's true that no one wants to watch 20 minutes of boring talking heads, but a lot can be done for lower budgets than are usually quoted.' Indeed, BT's in-house programme won an award in 1993 from the IVCA – the video industry's own association.

BT sells business television services to its corporate clients and it is obviously essential that BT should be seen to use what it sells. It is expanding its network to reach all office staff who deal with customers and already makes other programmes for its sales teams.

Broad bands

Up to this point, every BT product we have described transmits analogue signals along its telephone cables – the traditional waveform signals which echo the sound or picture waves created by the microphone or television camera. The threshold to the future comes when analogue signals are converted into digital signals, the on–off codes which represent the raw material of computer processing. BT is moving fast to introduce digital networks; its experimental cable service based at its R&D centre at Martlesham in Essex is just one such initiative. Already, BT uses its integrated services digital network (ISDN) – a broadband telecommunications link between different centres – for any number of applications, including employee communications. ISDN can transmit data as well as voice: BT uses it to send the made-up pages of the company newspaper directly to the reproduction house for printing. Most large organisations are today linked by ISDN – a digital telecommunications system with enough capacity to carry large volumes of data – or by satellite, which carries signals much more cheaply once the satellite receivers have been installed – or, indeed, by both.

Electronic junk mail

Where smaller organisations are concerned, the digital output of their computers can be converted, by use of modems, back into the analogue signals which any telephone line can transmit. In this way they can carry computer messages into remote sites and homes. The widest use of the telephone network is the Internet system whereby hundreds of thousands of computer users 'speak' to each other and exchange information; many small companies are now voracious users of Internet.

Brenda McAll draws attention to the danger of a new form of electronic junk mail. 'A manager can now copy a document to any number of people, and any of them can copy it on so that it eventually reaches thousands. No one asks themselves "do they really need to know this?" '. BT has strict rules controlling the broadcasting of messages to their senior managers, to stop their systems being clogged with unwanted messages.

Importantly, in the context of rapid communications, BT uses e-mail to send briefing notes to senior managers who are encouraged to cascade the information immediately to their own departments. BT is now experimenting with using the satellite channel for broadcast teletext. 'Providing the television monitors are always on,' says McAll, '– and somebody has to be responsible for seeing that they are! – and people get into the habit of looking at them at least once a day, teletext could make a big contribution to timely communications.' Looking further ahead, BT believes that in-house broadband systems could replace satellite-delivered television and deliver programmes to the desk top.

Desktop Television

And that is precisely what IBM's Desktop Television is designed to do. It offers all the advantages of BT's Business Television in that it transmits television programmes live via satellite to the buildings in which people work, offering the advantage of instant communication and an opportunity for people to interact with the speakers at the hub of the system.

IBM's Desktop Television offers the additional advantage of 'mix'n match'. The signal can be captured by the receiving stations and re-edited for their own purposes, with fresh text or images added, or sections deleted if they are not relevant to the interests of that outpost. That's because the signal is digital; indeed, Desktop Television can claim to be the first true corporate application of the digital highway, a video-on-demand system which allows staff to access interactive programmes they want to watch as and when they choose.

The first widespread application of Desktop Television is a joint venture with Independent Television News through which companies around Europe are fed a specially tailored news programme which arrives on their desks complete with text summaries and footnotes. They can either view the programme as it arrives off the satellite, or re-run it at their leisure. They can scroll or fast-forward through the sections they don't need to study in full, re-run others, and make their choice of material they might want to keep.

The IBM system is based on a read/write 'chip' developed in America for cable companies to enable their subscribers to select the programmes they want to watch and run them at the times they choose. It is able to receive a digital signal off either satellite or the network and compress it into the form which can be read by the computer. The chip records the incoming signal and instantly (a thirtieth of a second later) replays the programme on the computer screen – assuming, that is, that the user is available to watch it there and then. If not, or if the first-time viewer wants to study some sections in greater depth, then the complete programme has been stored in the memory.

Desktop Television offers both instantaneity – it makes it possible for most people to receive news immediately – and interactivity – the text, video and audio elements can be easily accessed and manipulated. Users can halt the process, review sections, ask questions, copy the sections they might want to keep and input their own data for others to consider.

IBM has already developed some ingenious applications of Desktop Television. Sothebys could transmit moving pictures of the treasures which are under the hammer along with text data to reinforce the sale – deeds of provenance, for example, and the history of the antique, plus the state of the bidding. Punters in any corner of the globe could submit their bids electronically through the same network by which they are receiving their signal from the auction room.

In the future, traders in dealing rooms could receive live newscasts direct on the computer screens they use to track the movement of markets; the same medium could be used to transmit corporate multimedia messages via the firm's computer server, which the traders could summon up at their convenience when the markets are quiet, and switch off when dealing hots up again. The same could be true for the controllers of power stations, for nurses and doctors on standby and for any number of others whose pattern of work is unpredictable and intermittent.

Like BT's Business Television, IBM's Desktop version is likely to be used mainly by very large and widespread organisations. Like Business Television, there are considerable costs in installing the telecommunications network and then in generating the multimedia programmes on a sufficiently regular basis to justify the capital costs. It may prove just as difficult to adjust ways of working to accommodate this powerful new communications tool.

Interactive multimedia

At this point, employee communications finds itself on the threshold of the same revolution which promises to transform entertainment media in the home. Once communications signals have been digitised, there is almost no limit to the flexibility which can be offered for the simple reason that the message can now be fed through a computer. The computer makes it possible for the facilitator or any user to access any part of the video, audio and text and then to reorganise, edit, re-route and interrogate the media. Above all, it enhances the quality of the signal.

For a decade and a half companies have been obliged to

screen recordings of motion picture programmes on cumbersome, low-quality equipment – the Video Home System (or VHS for short) originally developed by Japan's JVC for time-shifting television programmes for the convenience of family viewing. VHS records the video and audio signals on magnetic tape in the same analogue form as it was originally captured in the video camera or recording machine. The recording – especially the sound – is usually of poor quality; worse still, in the context of group viewings, it is impossible to move backwards or forwards on the tape except by spooling relatively slowly and blindly to the point where we hope the section we need is located.

Digital recordings of audio programmes have been commercially available for several years either on digital audio tape (DAT) or on compact discs (CDs). DAT offers the advantage that it is possible to re-record another performance over the existing copy, whilst CDs allow the user to move around the surface of the disc; the listener can switch tracks in an instant by feeding a new command into the control panel. Furthermore, CDs have proved rugged to the point of indestructibility, partly because digital messages carry redundancy of information. It is hardly surprising that CDs are now the dominant format for the sale of recorded music.

The reason why moving pictures have not until recently been recorded onto discs lies in the fact that it takes considerably more bandwidth to carry a visual signal than an audio one; there is more capacity on a spool of magnetic tape than on the surface of a compact disc. That's also the reason why video telephony has taken so long to appear – it requires not only several times as much cable capacity to carry the signal, but also vastly more switching equipment to route the visual message through the telephone exchanges.

Television is also a relative newcomer to the practice of transferring its analogue signals to digital. The first widespread use of digital video images came when clever companies like Quantel introduced digital effects into television – the first manifestations were 'special effects', the distortions and visual devices which played havoc with pop videos. Today, digital technology makes the recording and editing of video more flexible and subtle than was once dreamed possible.

The video image was digitised by sampling the curves of the analogue light waves and converting them to the traditional on–off message which computers understand. When analogue tapes are edited they lose quality with each 'pass': if the programme is edited too often the picture becomes technically unacceptable. Digital editing simply rearranges the digital signals with no loss of quality however many versions are made.

Compression

Once moving pictures could be digitised and handled by computers, a new weapon was available to the communicating organisation since video images could now in theory be handled as easily as text and every computer could carry them. However, there remained another challenge to be overcome if video were to be recorded onto compact discs – the fact that pictures occupy so much more bandwidth than sound or text messages. As digital video was gradually introduced during the early 1990s, the moving picture was at first of poor quality, with jagged, hesitant movements – in the tussle for space on the computer's memory, there was no room for full-screen, full-motion pictures. Instead, the moving picture was confined to a relatively small area of the screen – thus concealing the poor resolution of the images.

The next important development in the flexible use of moving pictures was compression, the technique of reducing picture signals to the smallest possible number of digital on–off messages whilst enabling the replay machine to reproduce the images in a close approximation to full motion and picture quality. Little by little, in the mid-1990s, the techniques of compression were improved to the point where 40, then 70 and, with some technologies, over 100 minutes could be captured on a single CD, whilst the resolution was improved sufficiently to occupy first half the screen and then the full screen.

The next challenge was incompatibility – the reluctance to buy one type of equipment for fear that it would be obsoleted if another standard came to dominate the market. The problem is familiar to those who bought Betamax video recorders in the 1980s, the superior technical quality of the Sony tape wasn't enough to save this format from being submerged beneath the marketing onslaught of Matsushita, whose VHS format soon became the standard in the market-place. The manufacturers of digital video equipment have moved quickly to forestall this danger.

Manufacturers agreed to a single technical standard. MPEG (Motion Pictures Expert Group) compression/decompression owes its origins to the karaoke player; it enables relatively low-powered equipment to play high quality video by the addition of special circuitry to the player, the FMV (full motion video) or MPEG card.

By now, personal computers had entered the act. Because the video signal is digital, and because many personal computers have colour screens and speakers, the PC can replace the television monitor. Leading up to the Christmas of 1994, television commercials hyped the new generation of PC, with built-in CD player, capable both of computing and of entertaining.

As with many technological innovations, the manufacturers targeted the domestic market before focusing on the office. Digitised moving pictures imprinted on compact discs were on sale in the American main street in early 1994 and in Britain six months later. In increasing numbers of living-rooms CD players screened movies, sporting events, pop concerts and children's programmes directly onto family television screens. They carried better picture and audio quality than their VHS predecessors, and they made it possible for the viewer to dip into the programme wherever they chose. This represented a considerable improvement on previous generations of linear media, but not a fundamental change in the process of conveying information in that the programmes were not mixed with other media and not designed in such a way that their audiences could interact with them in any meaningful way.

The important development for the corporate communicator lay in the fact that digitising moving pictures had opened the way to using them in the same way as any other form of computer data. As such, motion pictures could take their place as the latest and arguably the most powerful of the media which could be manipulated on the computer screen. The same disc could now carry not only text, still pictures and computer instructions but the full panoply of full-colour, full-motion moving pictures and sound. Most personal computers could be turned into television screens, complete with audio, by the insertion of an MPEG card. All at once, there was no need for companies to wheel in a video player linked to a television monitor and set it up in a conference room. The programme could be viewed on desktop computers anywhere in the building.

The interactive multimedia programme represented an alternative to the entertainment video CD which was already making inroads into the family living-room. The personal computer in the parents' study or the youngsters' den could now act as a glorified computer-based learning centre. Book publishers who had already produced text-only CD-ROMs now added moving-picture illustrations to reference CDs like *Grolier's Encyclopaedia* to provide 'living colour' to these coffee-table editions. At the same time, video publishers started adding text and discovery paths to television pro-grammes, especially documentaries and arts programmes which, up to now, had been sold as linear video tapes.

The first interactive multimedia programmes were published on CD, in a variety of formats ranging from Philips' pioneering CD-i through to rival products from the familiar group of Japanese and American manufacturers of electronic entertain-ment equipment. CDs offered economy – they are cheaper to reproduce than VHS tapes – and ease of handling. They are, however, almost certainly birds of passage. The same computer network which feeds business data around a wide-spread corporation can be used to feed communications media to the same terminals. A single server can store the multimedia programme on its powerful hard disc and provide simultaneous access to any number of users out there in the company's widespread outposts, each of whom can ask the computer to feed the information at a variety of speeds in different-sized chunks.

This offers to office networks the corporate equivalent of 'video-on-demand' – again, the domestic market provides the commercial impetus. The much-hyped 'digital superhighways' offer the domestic viewer the opportunity to summon up the programme of choice at the moment of convenience. In other words, each subscriber can command the system to start playing the movie or event he or she wants to watch; the vast number of pathways made possible by digital transmission allows each home to receive personal packages of pro-grammes, just as the telephone network allows individual conversations.

In the office, different workstations are similarly able to access the central server to feed the programme simultaneously; they can stop and start the show without affecting transmission to other people using the system at the same time. By using the computer network to feed communications packages to their staff, companies can avoid the disadvantages of video CDs.

The first is the need to buy the CD player itself. Second comes speed of access. For those who have been annoyed by the grinding slowness of VHS, the CD seems responsive and flexible; however, those who are used to the speed of today's computing find it annoying to have to brook delays whilst the CD waits for the head to lock onto the spinning disc at the correct point. Thirdly, the read-only memory of the CD means that images imprinted on the disc cannot be altered which can prove time-consuming and expensive when a corporate com-munications package needs updating.

The CD does offer some advantages over the computer

network. The first is its physical presence – the disc can be
stored on a shelf, its label can be eye-catchingly designed to
attract users and explain its contents – it offers the 'touchy-
feely' qualities familiar to those who collect books or records.
Where there is an advantage in delivering a tangible 'package'
of media, such as take-away discs and booklets for the
participants to take away and study at home, the CD may
prove favourite.

The man–machine interface . . .

The Quadrangle survey which we reported in Chapter 2
demonstrated how important it is in corporate communications
to use each of the media in the manner to which it is best
suited, and to mix them together in such a way that they
reinforce the facilitator and each other. It will by now be
apparent that by digitising all the media, this mixing and
reinforcing can be given finger-tip control. Each of the media
can be accessed, frozen, replayed and hard-copied at will and
in an instant. Multimedia programming can create journeys of
discovery, whereby the process of informing each individual
can move at the speed and with the emphasis which different
audiences demand.

By using techniques like IBM's Speak-up!, the media can
even contribute constructively to the message. The media can
be programmed to audit attitudes and reactions, measure
usage, embrace changes and additions. Importantly, they can
contribute to the process of 'layering' communication, allowing
the company to distribute information to each sector of its
audience in the form best suited to that audience and, if
necessary, encrypting any confidential data meant only for a
select few.

It is too soon to hail any of the new technology tools
reported in this chapter as the Messiah of employee communications. Each has its disadvantages – notably the cost of
generating the software for a really sophisticated interactive

multimedia roll-out programme. Furthermore, there is still a certain amount of thinking to be done and experiments to be conducted before it will be clear how best to adapt not only the media to the message but, more subtly, the communications process to the media.

For instance, the ideal use of multimedia is the so-called 'kiosk' application in which one person sits at a terminal, interacting with the programme in solitude, at his or her own pace. However, schools are waking up to the fact that they can't afford anything like enough multimedia stations to allow one-to-one learning and are developing methods of using multimedia in such a way that the whole class can view and interact in a group. In corporate communications, the same applies for different reasons.

If, as we believe, the most effective form of communicating complex change programmes lies with groups with a facilitator in charge, then it may be impractical to produce 'kiosk' versions of corporate programmes. The alternative is to produce a simpler form of communications package – the equivalent of a tape/slide/video session which offers the speed of response of digitised media but without the depth of interactivity needed for solitary study. The facilitator is able to respond to the wishes of the group by moving around the programme and screening the relevant text, video or audio when it is relevant to the discussion.

However, there may be some in the company who simply can't attend the group sessions – we have already alluded to jobs like those of the nuclear technician unable to leave the control room, the broker or dealer who can't leave the computer terminal, the shift worker who works unsocial hours, the export agent who can't be slotted into the scheduled meetings or the hospital worker who can't predict when the next break will occur. Alternatively, new recruits may join the company after the communications campaign has been completed. All of these will benefit from access to a terminal which provides access to interactive programmes which can respond to the users' questions or reactions. For these applications, the kiosk version will be invaluable especially if the issues raised in discussion and other recent developments have been recorded onto the package.

The future starts here

This chapter has attempted to raise the corner of the curtain on the potential of new technologies to improve the process of employee communications. It will probably be out of date before this book is published and should ideally be rewritten every week. Which, had it been feasible to publish it electronically instead of on paper, would most certainly be taking place . . .

 Count
the Cost

No matter what the cost of producing videos, printing news-letters or distributing audio tapes, there is little doubt that the most expensive element in any communications exercise is the management and employee time needed to make it work. It is also certain that well-planned and managed exercises can create real improvements in operating efficiency which more than justify these costs. However, even in well-intentioned and successful companies such as those featured in this book, it is a salutary thought to think that fewer than half of the exercises really achieved their potential and can be thought of as success stories.

The most common error that we can identify is the failure to define clear targets for communications and to spend too little effort at the planning stage and too little time in observing and measuring the effects of the process and adjusting programmes when they do not conform to plan. Companies which devote themselves to total quality management in all other areas of their operations often forget the basic principles when it comes to communicating with their staff.

Although every company and every message is different it is possible to see that the adoption of a structured approach to the design and management of communications can help to avoid costly mistakes and to increase the chances of success.

We have said earlier that employee communications is a developing science and some of the cases in this book have shown just how complex this field of endeavour can be. We can no more expect all managers to become communications experts than we would expect them to be expert in all aspects of law, corporate finance or information technology. Efficiency dictates that managers consult with experts within their own organisations or with consultants brought in for special projects. However, the costs of such exercises are considerably reduced if the managers themselves have carried out all the basic groundwork.

The approach which our rules suggest may appear deceptively simple – but it leads to a framework which can be used by managers to create a clear statement of their communications environment, the goals they wish to achieve and a project definition which can form the basis of the consultation with experts. Let us return to our five rules and develop a practical framework from them in the light of the experience of our case study companies.

Plot your route

As one might expect, there is a clear correlation between the apparent levels of success of communications programmes and the level of effort that was expended at the outset. The clearer the definition of the communications goal, the more specific the audience; the better defined the environment, the higher the likelihood of success. AEA Technology meticulously studied their own situation and measured it against the bench-marks of other similar organisations. This has not only helped develop the programme but has provided clear markers for measuring progress. Rover, Meridian and PW MCS were all working under time pressure and in turbulent times for their industries. However, the efforts that they spent in answering the key questions about their organisations at the outset has saved them time and money in the longer term.

Shoot the pianist

Although the existing corporate culture must be borne in mind when designing a programme, cultures are continually evolving and each message is different. Rather than simply repeating past practice the options should be considered afresh for each situation. BP and Rover took approaches which were radically different to the existing cultures within the organisations. It was these fresh approaches and the clear commitment of the managers promoting them which helped establish credibility. While the situation at Railtrack needed an urgent response, the willingness of the Railtrack management to select a fresh approach to their communications made a major impact which engaged the audiences and created and increased receptivity for the messages themselves.

Enrol your owners

There can be nothing worse than a communications programme where the key players at senior management level do not all believe in the messages themselves. Internal communications is one area where it is very difficult to fool all of the people any of the time. In the cases which we have looked at in this book, the most successful results have been achieved when all the essential communicators have not only felt that they believed in the message but that they also had a major role in its formulation. At BP Robert Horton created a dynamic team who championed the messages of Project 1990 and who created a distinctive shift in corporate beliefs towards a teamworking culture throughout the organisation. By enrolling a strong group of owners Horton made sure that the process could carry on after his departure. A similar strategy was adopted by Graham Day at Rover where he involved all senior management in the development of the new approach from the outset. By long-term attention to a communications process, Courtaulds were able to use their existing cell-briefing network and, through this, to make sure that line managers were fully committed to the success of the process.

Meridian Broadcasting started with a small strong management team who were absolutely committed to the development of a new style of broadcasting organisation. They had spent a long period defining the message and refining the culture that they wanted to develop in their staff. The problem was that the new staff themselves were coming from a wide variety of different backgrounds with different expectations and the whole process of organisational development needed to be accelerated. Even in these difficult circumstances, the clear commitment of the top management, who formed the basis of the small project team which designed and then facilitated the seminars for everyone joining the new company, paid off.

For each of these organisations, enrolling the owners at the outset developed a chain process which eventually made owners out of the audiences.

Encourage positive heckling

Possibly the most common error in internal communications is failing to ensure that the communication is a two-way process. This is essential for a variety of different reasons. If there is no direct mechanism for feedback there is no means of measuring whether the communication has been understood except through the long-term performance of the business – and that may be too late! Secondly, the feedback process itself is one of the elements of engagement in the process and can be highly motivating to the audience as well as reinforcing key concepts. Thirdly, some of the most essential information and effective suggestions for development can be locked up in the experience and thoughts of the audience (a review of Japanese internal communications systems shows that they recognise the 'limitations' of the bosses and make a strong positive effort to unlock the potential of employees through these processes).

This is not to say that it is always easy. The long-term corporate culture, which may have been strictly hierarchical and discriminated against people who spoke 'out of turn', may have developed a resistance to feedback. The original component companies that now form United Distillers were like this. UD had to make positive efforts to encourage feedback and to show employees that their views were valued. Openness formed an essential component of the core values that were a central element of the UD Way itself.

For PW MCS, feedback was almost the most essential part of the process. The senior partners needed to understand the views of the other professionals within the organisation. Sometimes feedback can be uncomfortable, but the demonstrated ability of management to cope with fair criticism in a positive manner has a unifying and motivating effect which reinforces a learning culture and enhances future progress.

Count the cost

How to avoid the dangers of spending too little or too much. Well, let us try to set out a clear template which will be the first stage in drawing up the blueprint for successful communications exercises.

How to count the cost

1   **Why are you planning a communications exercise at all?**
    Try to set down a simple statement of no more than 50 words which sets out the purpose of the exercise.

2   **What is the message?**

(a) **Who are you really trying to talk to?**
    Which are the key audience groups?
    How many people are there in the audience?
    Are they really only internal audiences or do you need to reach the extended enterprise?
    What are the special characteristics of these groups in terms of history, language, culture and location?

(b) **What are you trying to say?**
    What is the essence of the communication? Try to express the central message in less than 50 words.

(c) **What outcome do you expect from the exercise?**
    Try to specify measurable activities.

(d) **What are the time pressures and/or deadlines against which the communication must be achieved?**
    Note key dates, events, agreements that define the urgency of the exercise.

(e) What financial value can you place on the success of the exercise?
Try to think in terms of both overt and hidden benefits and to look at both short- and longer-term benefits.

(f) Bearing in mind the answer to 2(e), what budget is it reasonable to allocate?
Of course, there is no simple answer to this! Objectives should be achieved with the best cost efficiency possible. However, temper your answer here with a risk analysis of the cost of failure.

3   Who should be the messengers?
In answering this question you must pay attention to a number of key factors:

(a) What is the current communications culture?
Are there any recent surveys of the organisation that you can use or could you look at bench-marks of similar organisations and see how yours compares?

(b) Who will have credibility with the audience(s)?
Don't just write down the obvious list. Think laterally! There may be unlikely individuals or even those unpopular with management, who would be the most plausible communicators if they could be made into owners of the message.

(c) Who will be capable of delivering the message, or what training will they need?
Remember that there are many different factors involved in successful communications, varying from simple presentation abilities, through listening skills, abilities with presentation technology, to assertiveness training, meeting management and body language.

(d) What is the location structure, shift pattern and normal operating routine of the audience?
Try to identify whether there is a single environment that will always be used or whether there are many different options for which flexibility must be planned. Draw up a list of the techniques which must be ruled out because of the nature of the delivery environment.

(e) What are the time pressures on the audience?
Can the audience only be spared for short sessions or
is it possible to arrange for more extensive periods to
be devoted to a programme? This not only affects the
length and number of sessions but has a major effect
on the types of activity which can be used.

4   What type of programme will be most effective?
This is not about selecting the media but is rather
about the structure of the programme.

**(a) Is this a one-off communication or part of a longer-
term process?**
Try to identify any particular style elements or central
messages which must be incorporated in the design.

**(b) What links will this programme have into other
processes within the organisation?**
Be careful here to identify any activities which could
be thought of as competitive or disputed areas of
authority which may be problematic.

(c) How will action be stimulated?
Describe any specific ideas that you have to motivate
receivers to take action from the programme. Identify
any additional costs in financial or time terms that
these may incur.

**(d) What type of feedback do you need and how will it be
collected?**
It is also important here to think how respondents can
be reassured that their feedback is viewed as valuable
and that their voice is actually being heard and
stimulating a response.

**(e) Who will act as the focus and co-ordinator of the
exercise?**
Make sure that it is someone who is genuinely given
the freedom from other competing activities to concentrate on the programme.

(f) Where will the message be delivered?
Try to list all the characteristics of the planned
locations in terms of: size, technical facilities,
comfort, noise etc.

(g) Who will provide the resources for completing the programme?
This does not just mean the finance but includes issues like locations, additional human resources, transport and other support.

5   How will you ensure that your audience relates to and owns the message?

(a) Which key elements of the message will strike a personal cord with the audience?
List at least three elements which you believe will involve everybody.

(b) What steps can you take to involve the audience in constructing the communication?
Be realistic here and consider the levels of knowledge that the audience actually possesses or it is advisable for them to have before the communication takes place. As well as identifying the benefits, also look at the logistical and time problems that will be incurred through involvement.

(c) How will you reinforce the message?
Try to think of secondary activities which will clearly reward those who have taken the message on board and have acted accordingly.

(d) What channels for two-way communication will be possible?
Don't just look at existing mechanisms. Think about new opportunities such as e-mail, video conferencing or interactive business television.

6   What mechanisms will you set up to measure whether you have achieved your aims?
Are there ways in which you can link the results of the programme to clear business indicators that are part of the normal process? Should you plan a series of regular surveys or facilitated team discussion meetings?

If the next generation of managers learns to benefit from the experience, sometimes bitter, of the first, then fewer battles will be lost, fewer heroes suffer in the process, and more organisations will deserve the title 'communicating'.

▪️ Further Reading*

BUTLER S. 'Cutting and reshaping the core.' (On BP.) *Financial Times*, 20 March 1990

CHERRY C. 'Communication theory and human behaviour.' In A.H. Smith and R. Quirk, eds, *Studies in Communication*. London, Secker and Warburg, 1955

HANDY C. *The Age of Unreason*. Harmondsworth, Penguin, 1989

HARVEY-JONES J. *Making It Happen*. London, Collins, 1988

KANTER R.M. *The Change Masters: Corporate entrepreneurs at work*. London, Allen and Unwin, 1983

LEAVITT H.J. *Corporate Pathfinders*. Homewood, Illinois, Dow, Jones-Irwin, 1986

LORENZ C. 'Reshaping BP–A drama behind closed doors that paved the way for a corporate metamorphosis.' *Financial Times*, 26 March 1990

LORENZ C. 'Reshaping BP–Re-appraising the power base of the regional barons.' *Financial Times*, 26 March 1990

MABEY C. and MAYON-WHITE B. *Managing Change*. London, Chapman, 2nd edn, 1993

MILLER G.A. *Language and Communication*. Maidenhead, McGraw-Hill, 1963

NAISBITT J. and ABURDENE P. *Re-inventing the Corporation*. London, Guild, 1985

PETTIGREW A.M. and WHIPP R. *Managing Change for Competitive Success*. Oxford, Blackwell, 1991

ROETHLISBERGER F.J. and DICKSON W.J. *Management and the Worker*. Cambridge, Mass., Harvard University Press, 1939 (on the Hawthorne Effect)

SONY CORPORATION. *The Tools of the Trade – Research and scripting*. London, Sony, 1994 (a mixed-media course on creating videos or television programmes; details from: Declan Bermingham, Sony, The Heights, Brooklands, Weybridge, Surrey KT13 0XW)

TAYLOR B. and LIPPIT G. *Management Development and Training Handbook*. Maidenhead, McGraw-Hill, 1983

ZEIGARNIK B. 'Das Behalten erledigter und unerledigter Handlungen.' *Psychologische Forschungen*, Vol. 9, 1927

* None of the research reports described in Chapter 2 is readily available.

Index